Entrepreneurial Dynamics of Indian Diaspora in United Arab Emirates

Mili Sarkar

SP SHIPRA
SHIPRA

ISBN: 978-81-7541-714-4

First Published in India in 2014

Published by:
SHIPRA PUBLICATIONS
H.O.: LG 18-19, Pankaj Central Market, Patparganj,
Delhi-110092, Tel: 91-11-2223 5152, 2223 6152
Br.Off.: 4617/18, Ansari Road, Darya Ganj,
New Delhi-110002, Tel: 9650028065, 9810522367
E-mail: info@shiprapublications.com
www.shiprapublications.com

Dedicated to
My daughter – Paroma
My son – Parijat
and
My husband – Pinaki
for their unfailing support and faith in me

Acknowledgements

The book could not have been written without the support and encouragement of many people and institutions that I came across in the course my study, especially, Gautam Kumar Basu, who gave me much-needed valuable guidance. Much thanks and respect to him.

Special thanks also to Talmiz Ahmed, the Indian Ambassador to the UAE for 2007–2010, he provided me with required valuable information. He gave me the platform through which I got to meet and interview the renowned Indian diasporic entrepreneurs in the UAE.

My heartfelt thanks to the Strategic Research Centre of the UAE, for giving me permission to access study materials from the UAE Federation Library.

My thanks go to Siddhartha Shankar Ray, the librarian at the Centre for Studies in Social Sciences, Kolkata, Asim Kumar Nath, family and friends, Sathi and Bijon*da* for their invaluable support. My thanks are extended to my beloved student Thasneem Abubakar for helping me with typing and computer-related tasks and lending me moral support when needed.

Lastly, but not in the least, I would like to thank my daughter, Paroma, my son, Parijat, and my husband, Pinaki, for their unfailing support and faith in me. They provided me all the support and love that a wife and a mother could hope for from her family, and more.

Contents

1

Introduction

In the second half of the twentieth century, many countries have benefited themselves by acknowledging and utilizing the potentials of their respective diasporas. China and Israel were able to capitalize on the inflowing support from their respective diasporas to the maximum; traditional financial support in the form of remittances and private transfers was prudently utilized by them for various developmental purposes.[1]

The diasporic communities and entrepreneurs of a nation can play a crucial role in the economic development of their home country in various ways such as remittances, commercial activities, investment, skill circulation, networking and exchange of experiences. This study tries to study the entrepreneurial dynamism of and analyse various problems faced by the Indian entrepreneurs in the UAE. The contribution made by the Indians in the UAE proves that they are "global players". They carry with them not only financial assets, but also energy, talent, business ideas, etc. There is a need to understand their global connectivity that has enriched them in various fields giving them a competitive edge over the others.

India has not been successful in utilizing the true potential of its diasporas because since the early decades of the twentieth century the Indian economy has been functioning within an "inward looking" and an anti-market model of development. In order to attain sustained rapid growth, India needs to adopt a broader policy, allowing for more economic and political freedom. The slow growth rate has adversely affected the employment scene in India, and due to the lack of funds not much could be spend on anti-poverty programs either.[2] Critics may argue that India has already established itself as a world power and its growth rate is about to touch double digits, however, in reality, the Indian economy has not been capable of fully cascading the advantage of this growth down to its nuclear units or, even, to the society at large.[3] Poverty has been reduced, but not considerably enough. According to Bhagawati and Arvind Panagariya, the "type" of growth matters a lot in poverty reduction. Rapid growth in unskilled-labour-intensive industries that can create more opportunities for the poor has been neglected by India.[4]

There are currently 1.75 million Indian expatriates in the UAE who remit a huge amount in foreign exchange—nearly $2 billion—annually through regular banking channels.[5] A substantial part of this remitted amount could be utilized for poverty reduction and for many other productive purposes provided India succeeds in motivating the Indian diaspora to become developmental partners through appropriate incentive schemes for investment. These remittances mostly get used for consumption purposes in India and rarely go towards productive investment, yet this inflow has a significant positive multiplier effect on the economic growth and the investment pattern in India. According to Zachariah, Mathew and Rajan, "the larger the remittances the higher is the percentage decline in poverty."[6] Thus such a huge amount of money sent in by the Indian diaspora/diasporic entrepreneurs has a significant direct poverty-reducing and welfare-increasing effect.

The study tends to suggest appropriate incentive schemes designed for the recipients in order to mobilize these resources towards promoting enterprising growth in the low-skill-labour-intensive industry. In the following chapters this study will analyse in detail the contribution to the home as well as the host nation, other than remittances, made by these Indian diasporic entrepreneurs living in the UAE—the establishment of various enterprises in India as well as in the UAE, creation and catering to the demands of nostalgic trade, increase in export volume, and the enhancement of the bilateral relationship between India and United Arab Emirates. According to Prakash Jain, "globalisation has significant bearing on the formation of the Indian diaspora."[7] Margaret Walton-Roberts adds, "In the case of India, a significant cause and effect of globalisation are the million of emigrants, both temporary and permanent, that work beyond Indian borders."[8] With globalization, the number of emigrants has increased in the UAE, resulting in an increase in remittances. The volume of investment and trade across the border between India and the UAE has also increased. This study wants to highlight the Indian diaspora and entrepreneurs in the UAE as assets valuable to India.

The non-resident Indians in the United Arab Emirates are one of the wealthiest business communities in the Gulf region. According to the 2003 World Wealth Report of Merrill Lynch, there were 47,000 millionaires in the UAE and 52,000 in 2004; amongst whom, as was counted in 2003, there were 8,000 NRIs. As we have seen, the total amount remitted through official channels to India by the Indian diaspora in the UAE has been recorded to be nearly $2 billion per annum.[9]

The Indian diaspora and entrepreneurs in the UAE have played a crucial role in attracting FDI, promoting export of domestic products, creating joint ventures, etc. Thus they ought to be seen as global agents. Keeping these Indian entrepreneurs in the UAE at the centre of discussion, this study wants to iterate that any policy recommendation for economic development should incorporate entrepreneurship. Thus Indian entrepreneurs and the Indian diaspora of the UAE can actively partner with India in its developmental strategies.

Since the end of the Cold War, the meaning and significance of the term globalization has been an important topic of debate among scholars. No one can deny the fact that globalization has had some negative consequences in certain cases, increasing poverty, inequality, ecological degradation, etc. However, it will be unfair to discount the positive impacts that globalization has brought along with it. Proponents of globalisation argue that it has increased environmental consciousness which has resulted in the adoption of various programmes working towards environmental sustainability. In many cases global communication has facilitated the solution of humanitarian problems. Critics may argue that it has not resulted in an ideal economic order, but it has to be acknowledged that in some respects globalization has definitely promoted human welfare. But according to the 2006 Globalisation Index jointly published by A.T. Kearney and *Foreign Policy* magazine, the nations of Singapore, Ireland, Switzerland, USA, Netherlands, Canada and Denmark are the most globalized, while Egypt, India, Indonesia and Iran are the least globalized among the listed countries.[10]

Participation in a global economy can propel a country towards more success. Globalization has strengthened the ties among the nations. It has facilitated migration, the transmission of various ideas, trade, investment, remittances, technology transfer, and creation of newer types of organizations. As stated by Jean Dreze and Amartya Sen, "There is a worrying image of seclusion that has been invoked in many old Sanskrit texts in India (in *Hitopadesh*, *Ganapath*, *Prasannaraghava*, *Bhattikavya*, among others). This is the story of a frog that lives his whole life within a well and is suspicious of everything outside it. This 'kupamanduka'—the well-frog—has a worldview, but it is a worldview that is entirely confined to that well. The scientific, cultural and economic history of the world would have been very limited had we lived like well-frogs."[11] The cited analogy can only urge us to try and better understand the process and in doing so the benefits of globalization.

Globalization has brought the world much closer together, resulting in more transnational migration, transnational corporations, etc. Amartya Sen's advice to the Indian economy is to keep the "well-frog" attitude at bay. The benefits of globalization need to be seen through a broader perspective, such as the resultant interdependence among nations, and the broadened horizon of international trade and investment. According to Jean Dreze and Amartya Sen, "Over thousands of years, globalisation has shaped the progress of the world, through trade, travel, migration and dissemination of knowledge."[12] Living in an open society, it is much easier to take advantage of greater opportunities at a global level. Due to globalization, a huge number of entrepreneurs, professionals, traders, various skilled, semi-skilled and highly-skilled labourers were enabled to migrate to different parts of the world, particularly to the Gulf region, in search of better jobs, which Prakash C. Jain called "a piggyback ride on globalisation".[13] No doubt there are negative issues related to globalization, but if there is political will they can be avoided through proper utilization of the benefits from globalization which can be harnessed for the betterment of the underprivileged.

This study intends to draw the attention of researchers and policy makers in India towards the Indian diaspora/diasporic entrepreneurs in the UAE. These diasporas/diasporic entrepreneurs are a product of this global process as well as key role-player in this process. According to Prakash C. Jain, "Thanks to globalisation, the Indian entertainment industry which includes film, music, fashion, theatre, has expanded tremendously in the 1990s¼ the audience includes not only the non-resident Indians but also the Arab masses."[14] The Indian diaspora in the UAE has popularized Indian food, fashion and jewellery in the UAE market. They have an immense potential which can be harnessed for the benefit of India and the UAE. The study attempts to establish that though they may not be the main agent in this process but their potentials can certainly be utilized towards reduction of poverty, social inequalities and regional disparities. This is an area to which the Indian policy makers need to pay proper attention.

Objectives of the Study

There is an urgent need to tap the development potentials of Indians living in the UAE. Some reasons have been given below to show why. Firstly, the evidence suggests that the amount of remittances sent by them to India is quite high. Secondly, India should try and make the most of the available advantage in the UAE market, thanks to the Indian entrepreneurs in the UAE who can readily act as agents in this process. Thirdly, it is necessary that every state in India should make an endeavour to acquaint their people with the achievements of the Indian entrepreneurs in the UAE; they can be future role models to entrepreneurs in India as well as play a key role in the "cross fertilization of ideas".

One can agree with the remark by Prakash C. Jain that this ignorance about the UAE-resident Indian diaspora is "a major gap in our understanding of a segment of worldwide Indian diaspora that has so far been least researched."[15] The main objective of this study is to shed some light on the various aspects of the Indian diaspora in the UAE, with special focus on the Indian entrepreneurs within that diaspora. In the following chapters we shall discuss in detail their successes, the challenges they faced and the role they have played in the growth of the Indian economy. An attempt has also been made to articulate the important hypotheses supported by this research that in the end may give some scope for further research in this field.

Review of Literature

A body of literature on diaspora and entrepreneurship is presently available. However, it is necessary to note that there is no literature available on the Indian entrepreneurs in the UAE, besides the pioneering work, titled *Non–Resident Indian Entrepreneurs in the United Arab Emirates* by Prakash C. Jain.[16] Migration and developmental literature is presently dealing with the contribution of diaspora to various developmental activities and addressing various possible ways to maximize the potential of diasporas.

De Haas[17] analysed various strategies developed by the host countries that target the diasporas to make them contribute more towards the development of the host countries. He put together case studies from Netherlands, United Kingdom, France, Belgium, Germany, Italy, and Spain. His study suggests that it is necessary on the part of the governments to reduce the cost of remittance. A good investment climate will channelize the remittances towards productive investment. This study further suggests that "brain circulation" programmes and setting up of small enterprises with support from the governments will increase the interest of the diasporas in becoming a partner in development; that collective developmental projects led by diasporas should be encouraged by the government; that the "co-founded projects" introduced by the Dutch government is an example of successful governmental support to network and capacity building amongst the diasporas and should be followed by other governments. Hence, the governments should acknowledge the "unique strength of diasporas".

Ratha[18] stresses that workers' remittances are an important source of developmental finance for developing countries. This study argues that the inward flow of remittances will bring about a positive impact on the growth, investment and income distribution for the recipient countries. It analyses various measures which can be implemented by the industrialized and developing countries to increase the inflow of these remittances. According to this study, a country can attract more remittances by encouraging international migration. It also remarks that remittances are the second largest source of direct income after FDI. The policy recommendations suggested by this study are: a) the need to create a strong financial infrastructure; b) policy improvement regarding foreign exchange control; c) reduction of remittance transaction costs through creation of competition among the money-transfer agents; d) easy access to banking service through migrant workers; e) better investment climate in the recipient country.

Johnson and Sedaca[19] have given a detailed representation of the various diaspora mechanisms which can be utilized for reduction of poverty and generation of growth, provided the diasporic community is allowed to act as a key stakeholder. They have analysed diaspora-related developmental programmes from the standpoint of remittance, diaspora business linkage, collective remittance for community development, and diaspora-driven trade, investment, and knowledge-transfer mechanisms. Johnson and Sedaca see the diaspora as the "first movers" who can generate investment in their home country. Emphasizing the knowledge-transfer mechanism, they comment that professional diasporas can share their knowledge with others through their network. They further advise that various financial instruments such as investment funds, sovereign diaspora bonds, etc., be introduced to mobilize the diasporic resources towards public and private sector. The authors conclude that proper utilization of the above can help produce more benefit from the diasporas.

Lowell and Gerova[20] shed some light on important diaspora mechanisms such as "optimal brain strain, return migration, financial instruments, entrepreneurial investments, hometown associations, migration and trade, and professional diaspora networks. The study presents some case studies from India, Taiwan, China and Korea, and on the basis of these it argues that returning migrants bring with them various new skills learnt in another country. The study emphasizes the urgent need for systematic cataloguing of various mechanisms through which the diaspora can foster development. The study argues that low-, medium-, and highly-skilled expats can create enterprises. The low-skilled expats have a greater interest in entrepreneurship as it provides them with an alternative to low-paid jobs. On the other hand, highly-skilled entrepreneurs normally engage themselves in capital-intensive business and bring heavy returns to the home country. The medium-skilled entrepreneurs generate many technological innovations by transferring their knowledge. The study also comments that most of the existing literature on this subject ignores the level of skill and gives feedback which is not always acceptable. The main challenges to investment by the diaspora are an unstable economy and political climate and lack of appropriate protection. This study concludes that there is a need for further research on the contributions of the diaspora to economic development assessed through live field studies rather than dated, static information derived from the existing body of literature.

Hugo[21] opines that modern transportation and communication systems have minimized the distances between nations. This has facilitated the quick flow of information between diaspora and potential movers resulting in an increase in foreign direct investments (FDIs) and improved reception of various kinds of developmental assistance from the migrants.

Newland[22] states that the diaspora may prove to be an important resource for poverty reduction and suggests that it is necessary to encourage such trans-nationalism where the diaspora can act as the engine of economic development. Remittance can be put to use to finance education and women's empowerment. In order to increase development and the impact of remittance, USAID should consider a strategy which should include both regulated and non-regulated MFIs as remittance agents as these institutions have the maximum capacity to fulfil the different financial needs of remittance-receiving households. The unregulated NGOs have successfully rendered many services to the households, helping to further increase the developmental impact of remittances. There is a need to increase the government's institutional capacity to address the issues related to remittances and the monetary institutions transferring these remittances. Thus a concrete policy should be adopted for maximum utilization of remittance for development.

Orozco[23] provides a broad presentation of the multifaceted impact of the diasporas on economic development. He has conducted his research in the Latin American and Caribbean countries and lists a set of five "T"s related to all diasporas of the world—tourism, transportation, telecommunication, trade (nostalgic), and transmission of remittance. Tourism, to which the diasporas contribute a lot, is the major money-making source for all developing countries. The regular visits paid by the diasporas to their homelands generate money for the home as well as the host country. They also visit holiday destinations like the non-national tourists. Orozco mentions that the US airlines generate a lot of money from such travelling. Diasporic travel has also facilitated changes in transportation infrastructure—airports, bus services, taxis, etc. The regular telecommunication of the diasporic groups with their family and business associates have greatly benefited the telecommunications sector. The diasporic group prefers the taste of its own cultural food, household items, etc., and this demand for nostalgic goods gives rise to the nostalgia trade. As a result, now there are many ethnic stores all over the world catering to such demands. Finally, the most important contribution is the remittances sent to families back in the home country.

Kathleen Newland and Hiroyuki Tanaka[24] suggest that diasporic entrepreneurship can contribute a lot to the home country in terms of creating business, generating employment opportunities, stimulating innovation, strengthening social capital, and mobilizing political and financial capital. This study found an incapacity on the part of the major developing countries to take advantage of opportunities from their diasporic entrepreneurs; very few countries were successful in attracting investments from their diasporic entrepreneurs. Not all among these entrepreneurs have the capacity to contribute to economic development. This study categorizes entrepreneurs as being of two types: "necessity entrepreneurs" and "opportunity entrepreneurs". Necessity entrepreneurs, often unable to find any other work, create small businesses to satisfy their own demands and have little power to contribute towards the economic development of their home country; they, however, help reduce the "overt unemployment" situation back home by migrating away for work. Opportunity entrepreneurs on the other hand exert a direct positive impact on the economic development of the home country with their capacity to recognize and take advantage of newer markets in the world. The study suggests that government programmes should include not only the "value-adding firms", but should consider both types of entrepreneurs. The study also suggests that pro-diaspora government policies, good governance, favourable social and cultural attitudes towards entrepreneurs, easy access to financial institutions, can trigger investment motivation among these diasporic entrepreneurs. Governments, various institutions, diasporic organizations and civil society groups can work together to help diasporic entrepreneurs remove obstacles in the path of investment and encourage further investment.

Lucas[25] notes that the most important asset possessed by the diaspora is their transnational social network. The capability of the diaspora to generate opportunities and transfer knowledge depends on the frequency and quality of their interpersonal interactions. Lucas attached more value to the education and skill levels of the diaspora which give them the capacity to increase trade through their network and act as leaders, motivating others to invest in their home country.

Prakash C. Jain[26] has carried out a pioneering piece of research in his book, titled *Non-Resident Indian Entrepreneurs in the United Arab Emirates*, already referred to, that gives a clear understanding of the non-resident Indians in the UAE, who are among the richest business communities in the Gulf. Jain argues that the contribution of these successful Indian entrepreneurs in the UAE towards India has been immense, however, they have not got the attention due them from policy makers as well as researchers in India. Since 1970, these entrepreneurs have made a fortune by investing in the UAE within a business climate that is supportive towards entrepreneurial growth. He acknowledges the role of the first wave of Indian émigrés who laid the foundation for this process of success. He further comments that this diverse and talented group of Indian entrepreneurs in the UAE has made immense contributions to various fields in the UAE. In this work Jain also appreciated the institutional network laid down by the old as well as modern entrepreneurs that has helped foster the bilateral relationship between India and UAE.

Furthermore, in his article "An 'Incipient' Diaspora: Indians in the Gulf Region"[27] Jain represents the sociological characteristics of the Indian migration to the Persian Gulf region. Following Myron Weiner he characterises the Indian diaspora as an "incipient diaspora". He states that these diasporic Indians are not immigrants in the true sense, however, they continue to stay in the Gulf for a long period of time without any citizenship rights; their process of migration has been "transitory and circulatory" in nature. He defines the relationship between India and the UAE as "symbiotic". Indians depend on the UAE for economic gain, whereas the Arab states are dependent on Indian labourers who are law-abiding, docile, hardworking and disciplined. He finally comments that the status of Indians in the UAE is as non resident Indians (NRIs).

K.C. Zachariah, E.T. Mathew and S. Irudaya Rajan[28] have represented a historical account of emigration from the state of Kerala. They observe that ever since 1970 a large number of Keralites have been migrating to take up various opportunities in the Gulf states. The effect of this migration has brought about changes in the economic, political, social and religious lives of these people. The authors admit that lack of data on external migration from India has limited the scope of research in this field. This study was based on usual methods of migration analysis, for example, cross tabulation, regression analysis, etc. It recommends reduced negativity towards migration and advocates policies favouring it to enhance the developmental impact of migration. This study narrows down the various Indian migratory trends to the basic two: short-term or long-term migration. The short-term prospects need an urgent enhancement of skills by the Keralite workers, whereas for the long-term prospects, the study suggests the adoption of a more globalized outlook by the educational system in Kerala.

K.C. Zachariah, B.A. Prakash and S. Irudaya Rajan's article "Aspects of Indian Labour Diaspora in the UAE"[29] which appears in Prakash Jain's book. is a survey-based research study on the Indian labour diaspora in the UAE .The study was conducted through three major cities—Dubai, Abu Dhabi and Sharjah and clearly portrays the employment and working conditions of Indian emigrants in the UAE. It describes the various facilities enjoyed by them, and gives a brief presentation on the employment structure in the UAE wherein the tertiary sector is predominant. The paper also analyses other important aspects such as the immigration policy of the UAE and the future demand pattern of labour in the UAE.

Fatma Al-Sayegh[30] gives an interesting representation of the merchant's role in Dubai's developmental process in her article on how the merchant class operated in the Gulf since the pre-oil era. Taking Dubai as a case study, she examines not only the economic role played by these merchants but also some other roles assumed by them. Dubai, also known the "city of merchants", was dominated by Indians and Iranians before the twentieth century. Possessing a strong financial power, this merchant class was the main financier to the pearling industry thriving on the Trucial coast, and hence they enjoyed a special position in society. They were a part of the advisory board—*majlis*. This article gave an interesting and detailed account of the rise of this merchant class in the Gulf, their involvement in the decision-making process in the pre-oil era, and their key role in designing the future of the Arab-Gulf states.

Myron Wiener, in his "International Migration and Development: Indians in the Persian Gulf,"[31] demonstrated the first systematic approach towards representing the diaspora in the Persian Gulf. Weiner here comments that the small oil-producing states, including the United Arab Emirates, solved their man-power and labour shortage problems by recruiting temporary workers from outside. These Gulf states, which are mostly monarchical, did not however give permanent resident status to migrants. The monarchy's fear of probable "political erosion" dues to the migrants was the main reason for this strategy. Weiner also states that these states in turn favoured their own nationals and tribes to the maximum with their state welfare programs. This study gives a clear description of the migrants from south Asia and India. Weiner criticizes the developmental programme undertaken by the Gulf States in this article, and in doing so observes the social order through a divide: the consumption-oriented native population; and production-oriented migrant population. The migrants, an indispensible part of the Gulf economy, stay within their own social group as they are not permanent residents and are considered subordinate to the nationals. Despite all the negative factors associated with their temporary stay, the lucrative opportunities attract the migrants to this region. Finally Weiner comments, the fate of the Indian diaspora depends a lot upon on the Indo-Gulf relationship.

Anand Mullo's *Voices of the Indian Diaspora* is a unique collection of contemporary as well as classical Indian diaspora literature from all over the world.[32] Mullo in this book emphasizes the huge potential possessed by these Indian diasporas. Some of the suggestions he articulates in this book for India on its road to becoming a world power include the need for visionary leadership, development of social infrastructure, improvement in work culture, education, and individual and social responsibility. He advises the network of diaspora to take into consideration the various objectives and successes of the Global Organisation of People of Indian Origin (GOPIO). The latest information regarding various issues and political situations in many countries such as Fiji, Trinidad and Tobago, Guyana, has found representation in this book. Mullo also analyses the various reasons behind the successes and failures of the Indian diasporas in their host countries and states his belief that the success of PIO (People of Indian Origin) is dependent on a good and close diasporic community. He advises the diasporas that in order to rediscover their Indian-ness, they should derive inspiration from their immigrant forefathers and try to acknowledge their struggle and contribution. In order to develop a closer link between India and themselves, he further advises, they should look at themselves though the "diasporic mirror" which will enable them to withstand various challenges.

Ram Buxani is a famous Indian businessman belonging to the Sindhi community who has been residing in Dubai for many decades. *Taking the High Road*,[33] his autobiography, reflects the spirit of entrepreneurship inherent amongst people from the Sindhi community. According to Buxani, the extraordinary skills possessed by the people of this community, their courage, tenacity and determination is what made them, as he states, "people destined to succeed". He characterizes the Sindhis as a truly an international community, one that does not suffer from any biases relating to caste, race, religion and nationality. He appreciates the role of the Sindhi women who provide emotional support and keep intact the cultural identity of India. He comments that there are many issues related to non-resident Indians that need to be tackled by the government. The attitude towards the NRIs, according to him, was not favourable as they were projected as "selfish, loud and unpatriotic", however, he acknowledges, since the wake of liberalization and globalization in India, attitudes towards the NRIs have started to change. He mentions his contribution in abolishing the Estate Duty in India. This autobiography gives a thorough account of the transition of Dubai towards modernization, besides the struggles and suffering faced here by the early wave of Indian diaspora.

Research Questions

On the basis of the review of literature that has been presented above, the study will address the following specific questions:

- What is the type of Indian diaspora to the UAE?
- What type of challenges did the emigrants face?
- What special attributes do they have which have made them so successful?
- What sort of contribution did they make towards India as well as UAE?
- What sort of policy from the home and host countries can maximize the utilization of their potentials?
- What role did they play in enhancing bilateral relations between India and UAE?

In what respects can the Indian diaspora/entrepreneurs in the UAE be a valuable asset to India and can they be utilized successfully as partners in development?

Hypotheses Used

The main research hypothesis revolves around the Indian diaspora/entrepreneurs in the UAE. They are potential development resources to India. This study argues that they can play a significant role in the process of economic development in India and examines how their potentials could be fully utilized for furthering development by India. Broadly speaking, the following two hypotheses can be stated:

Firstly, being an incipient diaspora, the Indian diaspora in the UAE can potentially be a part of the developmental process in India.

Secondly, the Indian entrepreneurs in the UAE are a strategic asset to India.

Based on a field study in the UAE and an assessment of the role played by Indian diaspora/diasporic entrepreneurs in the UAE, it appears that their collective nationalistic attitude is stronger than the Indian diasporas in other countries, as they are only too aware of the temporary nature of their stay in the UAE. They are engaged in various philanthropic activities, and in need they have always stretched out their helping hands towards India. Appropriate policies geared towards them will probably bring about desired results. Efforts will be made in the following sections to see whether or not the two hypotheses mentioned above are correct.

METHODOLOGY AND RESEARCH STRATEGY

***Survey Questionnaire and Case Studies*:** The field study took more than a year. In order to gain accurate information the author conducted interviews with the Indian diaspora and a few entrepreneurs in the UAE. The research strategy included a structured questionnaire, with open-ended questions permitting the entrepreneurs to express their views. This face-to-face exchange of views and the ensuing discussions helped bring to the surface a lot of inside information regarding many issues which were originally not included in the questionnaire. Thus, these face-to-face interviews certainly enriched the quality of this study.

Formal questionnaires were initially sent out to many, individuals and companies, through e-mails, only a few of those that were returned were completed correctly. To avoid this problem, and to gain the correct opinions, the questionnaire was restructured in another format. The main difficulty faced was to get the approval from the owners of the firms. Some of the companies responded with various excuses to avoid participating in the survey, whereas many of the companies did not reply at all. Again, with those firms that agreed to the interviews, it was very difficult to get an appointment. Many times interviews got postponed because the owners were busy with other activities or out on overseas tours. However, by and large most of the owners were willing to express their views during the interviews. Every effort was made through personal contacts and friendly channels to reassure them. Despite constrained resources, useful data was collected in the end. This study managed to gather the required information from the semi-structured and multiple choice questions, as well as the relatively open-ended interviews.

While the main aim of the questionnaire-based survey was to gather opinion from a large sample of people, the case studies provided a deeper understanding of the issues related to the present study. The material for the case study was gathered through direct and in-depth interviews, company profiles and published documents. Five case studies have been presented as role models later in this study. Face-to-face communication with the owners and visits paid to the workplaces provided extra information related to the study.

In order to check the reliability of materials collected from the survey and for the case studies, they were rechecked with published sources such as:

a) Company profiles and annual reports;
b) Directories;
c) Published biographies of entrepreneurs;
d) Reports and articles from Newspapers—such as *Gulf News*, *Khaleej Times*.

The study put more emphasis on qualitative analysis than on quantitative analysis. In order to gain variety in opinion, potential respondents were chosen from various sectors. The required data was collected amidst various constrains. The empirical findings of this study have been presented later, in the sixth chapter. Since the aim of the study is to align the resources possessed by the Indian diaspora/diasporic entrepreneurs with the economic growth of India, some emphasis is laid on the requisite policy formulations to support such an alignment.

Other Sources of Information: At the initial level, the study relied heavily on the questionnaires and matter gathered from interviews, however, later on, in order to gain further qualitative information, a number of informal contacts were made by the author at various levels such as the Chamber of Commerce, the Ministry of Information and Culture, the Indian Embassy, the Emirates Centre of Strategic Studies and Research (ECSSR), the Cultural Foundation of UAE, etc. Other sources include:

a) Members of various social organizations in the UAE such as the Indian Social Centre, Malayalee Samajam, Kerala Social Centre, etc.
b) Extensively searched literature such as various articles, surveys, academic journals, reports, bulletins, directories and periodicals.
c) Field visits to a number of industrial areas such as Mussafah in Abu Dhabi, the Free Trade Zone (FTZ) in Dubai, etc.

Scope and Limitation: The most important problem the researcher faced was in collecting the various information and data regarding target population. Unfortunately data and information is very limited in the UAE. During research the author found that there is a lack of comprehensive data in this field. Most of the available documents are in Arabic; even the Chamber of Commerce of Abu

Dhabi deals with everything in Arabic. Hence, the study had to rely heavily on face-to-face interviews and surveys on Indian diasporas. During these face-to-face interactions, some direct questions were asked to gather as much of quantitative information and personal views as was possible. The study acknowledges the fact that the findings are constrained, however, special care was taken to represent the data so as to best serve the purpose of this study.

The geographical area of survey included three main cities in the UAE—Abudhabi, Dubai and Sharjah. Being a lady researcher, the author faced many problems working against the backdrop of a traditional Muslim society. In order to minimize the magnitude of such limitations, the author had to depend on relatively fewer case studies than she would have wished to enrich the study.

***Survey Sample*:** The survey participants were chosen at random, although the main intention was to gather a variety of information from people belonging to various disciplines to get a wider coverage. The entrepreneurs were selected from various backgrounds. This study does not claim perfect representation of the entire Indian diasporic population present in the UAE. In the end, the selection was made by the author keeping in accordance with the element of convenience. The various associated limitations shall keep the author from claiming the study as a statistically correct report. About the major issues represented in this study, the majority was reached through a broad consensus. This is so because most of the respondents based their views and ideas not only on their present experiences in the UAE but also, their past experiences in their country of origin which helped them analyse every question in an appropriate way. A detailed account of the findings of the survey has been presented in the following section.

Conclusion

The main objective of this study is to explore the potential of the Indian diaspora/diasporic entrepreneurs in the United Arab Emirates, as well as to investigate into their contributions towards their home and host country. This study intends to fill in the gap that keeps us from fully understanding the roles they play and can potentially play with respect to India and the UAE. The empirical findings from the field research conducted in the UAE in the form of a questionnaire survey were deduced with an intention to better understand their importance as well as their hopes, and in doing so, help India to devise favourable policies to optimize their contributions and also align them as partners in development. This study in its entirety, also hopes to broaden the scope for further research.

ENDNOTES

1. Lev M. Freinkman, "Role of the Diasporas in Transition Economies: Lessons from Armenia," *Cuba in Transition* 11 (August 2001): 332, http://lanic.utexas.edu/project/asce/pdfs/volume11/freinkman.pdf (accessed March 17, 2010).
2. Jagdish N. Bhagwati and Charles W. Calomiris, *Sustaining India's Growth Miracle* (New York: Columbia University Press, 2008), 5.
3. *Ibid.*, 19.
4. *Ibid.*
5. Prakash C. Jain, *Non-Resident Indian Entrepreneurs in the United Arab Emirates* (New Delhi: Manak Publications, 2010), inside front cover jacket flap.
6. K.C. Zachariah, E.T. Mathew, S. Irudaya Rajan, *Dynamics of Migration in Kerala: Determinants, Differentials and Consequences* (New Delhi: Orient Longman, 2003), 257.
7. Jain, *Non-Resident Indian Entrepreneurs*, 12.
8. Margaret Walton-Roberts, "Globalisation National Autonomy and Non-Resident Indians," *Contemporary South Asia* 13, No. 1 (March 2004): 53–69.
9. Jain, *Non-Resident Indian Entrepreneurs*, 179.
10. A.T. Kearney, as cited by Biswanath Ghosh and M.V. Pylee, in *Indian Ethos and Values* (New Delhi: Vikas Publishing House, 2010), 63.
11. Jean Drèze and Amartya Sen, *India: Development and Participation* (New Delhi: Oxford University Press, 2002), 342.
12. *Ibid.*
13. Jain, *Non-Resident Indian Entrepreneurs*, 39.
14. *Ibid.*, 38.
15. Ibid., inside front cover jacket flap.
16. See endnote 5 for publication details.
17. Hein de Haas, "Engaging Diasporas: How Governments and Development Agencies can support Diaspora Involvement in the Development of Origin Countries," International Migration Institute, Oxfam Novib (June 2006).
18. Dilip Ratha, "Worker's Remittances: An Important and Stable Source of External Development Finance," *Global Development Finance* 2003, World Bank Report (December 2003).
19. Brett Johnson and Santiago Sedaca, "Diasporas, Émigrés and Development: Economic Linkages and Programmatic Responses," U.S. Agency for International Development (USAID), Washington, D.C., Trade Enhancement Service Sector (TESS) Project, CARANA Corporation (March 2004): 81, http://pdf.usaid.gov/pdf_docs/PNADC365.pdf (accessed March 17, 2010).

20. B. Lindsay Lowell and Stefka G. Gerova, "Diasporas and Economic Development: State of Knowledge," Institute for the Study of International Migration, Georgetown University, Washington, DC, World Bank Report (September 13, 2004), http://siteresources.worldbank.org/INTGEP2006/Resources/LowellDiaspora.doc (accessed March 17, 2010).
21. G. Hugo, "Migration and Development: A Perspective from Asia," *Migration Research Series* 14, IOM (November 2003).
22. Kathleen Newland and Erin Patrick, "Beyond Remittance: The Role of Diaspora in Poverty Reduction in their Countries of Origin," Migration Policy Institute, Department of International Development (July 2004), http://www.migrationpolicy.org/pubs/Beyond_Remittances_0704.pdf (accessed March 17, 2010)
23. Manuel Orozco, *Remittances to Latin America and the Carribean: Issues and Perspectives on Development*, Organization of American States Report (September 2004).
24. Kathaleen Newland and Hiroyuki Tanaka, "Mobilizing Diaspora: Entrepreneurship for Development," Migration Policy Institute, U.S. Agency for International Development (USAID), Washington, D.C. (October 2010).
25. Robert E.B. Lucas, "International Migration Regimes and Economic Development," EGDI seminar Report, Executive Group on Development Issues, Stockholm, Sweden (May 13, 2004), http://www.egdi.gov.se/seminar6.htm (accessed March 17, 2010).
26. Jain, *Non-Resident Indian Entrepreneurs*; see endnote 5 for publication details.
27. Prakash C. Jain, ed., "An 'Incipient' Diaspora: Indians in the Gulf Region," in *Indian Diaspora in West Asia: A Reader* (New Delhi: Manohar Publishers, 2007)
28. Zachariah, Mathew and Rajan, *Dynamics of Migration in Kerala*; see endnote 6 for publication details.
29. K.C. Zachariah, B.A. Prakash and S. Irudaya Rajan, "Aspects of the Indian Labour Diaspora in the United Arab Emirates," in *Indian Diaspora in West Asia: A Reader*, ed. Prakash C. Jain, Chap. 9, 205–36 (New Delhi: Manohar, 2007).
30. Fatma Al-Sayegh, "Merchants' Role in a Changing Society: The Case of Dubai, 1900–90," *Middle Eastern Studies* 34, No. 1 (January 1998): 87–102.
31. Myron Weiner, "International Migration and Development: Indians in the Persian Gulf," *Population and Development Review* 8, no. 1 (March 1982): 1–36, reprinted in *Indian Diaspora in West Asia,* ed. Prakash C. Jain (New Delhi: Manohar, 2007).
32. Anand Mullo, *Voices of the Indian Diaspora* (Delhi: Motilal Banarsidass, 2007).
33. Ram Buxani, *Taking the High Road* (Dubai: Motivate Publishing, 2003).

2

History of United Arab Emirates

This chapter looks into the history of the United Arab Emirates with the intention to clearly present the realities of the Indian diasporic entrepreneurs working there. Contemporary UAE has become a centre of attraction to the outside world due to the magnificent endeavourer through which it was able to transform a sustenance economy to the position where it can place itself as one of the most developed nations of the world. It has been able to reconstruct its social and economic condition which is at par with the most advanced nations of the world. Today it is one of the richest oil-producing countries of the world, supplying oil to all industrialized nations. But this road to success has not always been smooth. This present UAE which has been able to place itself on the world stage did not draw much attention from the world before the discovery of oil. To better understand this transformation, one has to investigate the history of the UAE. An attempt will be made in this chapter to shed some light on the various aspects of the UAE's development.

Ancient Period

Various archaeological findings suggest that people first arrived in the UAE tens of thousands of years ago. Scattered flint tools have been found in the deserts and also near the mountains which provide evidence of the presence of inhabitants in this region. It is believed that the climate of the UAE was previously wetter and more humid than the present day. Until 3000 BCE, this area was very humid, facilitating immigration.[1] The people of the UAE are basically of Arab origin.[2] Recent studies conducted by scientists reveal that the Arabian Peninsula was originally a part of Africa, separating and merging with the Asian continent. Thus Arabia became a connecting link between Africa and Asia and acted as a land bridge between these two continents.[3] Due to scarcity of sufficient materials it is very difficult to arrive at a conclusion as to when and how people first came to this region.[4] The local population of the present day UAE is tribal. Lorimer remarked that "indeed the country is tribally one of the most composite and perplexing".[5]

Structure of Tribal Society

Any analysis of UAE history will be incomplete without a proper understanding of the nation's tribal character. According to Rosemarie Said Zahlan, "Until the very recent past, the tribal structure of the populations dominated political and social life.... The tribal society of the Gulf States consisted of the Bedouin (*bedu*) and settled people (*hadar*). The *bedu* roamed the inland areas in search of grazing and water, while the *hadar* settled the coastal villages and towns and became the overwhelming majority."[6] Frauke Heard-Bay argued that the retention of tribal structure throughout the country is to be seen from the standpoint of economic diversification. Until the discovery of oil, the scarcity of natural resources prompted the people of this region to take up various economic activities such as camel-breeding, pearling, farming, fishing or sailmaking. She observes, "Before the advent of oil, the population could generally not afford to segregate as settled inhabitants, into merchants, fishermen and pearlers on the coast, agriculturists in the fertile oases and wadis and other groups exclusively tending their animals. Because such specialization was for most families throughout the ages impracticable, social separation into occupational groups did not take place either."[7] The tribesmen were dependent on one another not only for mutual defence against their enemies but also for the tribal spirit that played a key role in the functioning of their society. According to Edward Henderson, "not only kinship but the spirit of selflessness, chivalry, readiness to self sacrifice which is called *muruwah,* is the key."[8] Here, allegiance is the main determinant in the choice of leadership. In a true tribal society, a sheikh belongs at the top of the tribal structure and if his decisions are not acceptable to the tribe he receives constant warnings from senior responsible tribesmen. Thus it is seen that the unsupported decision of the tribal chief is not considered an ultimate verdict. Edward Henderson commented, "There is no doubt that there is something very glamorous about a really effective tribal leader: he is on his own; he has no bureaucracy to support him; he may or may not have recourse to a *Qadi* for a trickier religious and legal problem which he has to face; he is himself on trial every minute of every day because his people have chosen him and will only continue to support him if he measures up to their requirements."[9]

Tribal organization is basically hierarchical in nature. The level of hierarchy starts with the family, then the section, the clan, the tribe and sometimes the tribal confederation. The tribal chief was the main source of authority who was chosen by the elders on the basis of various qualification such as bravery, honesty and hospitality. Each state was composed of various tribes and thus tribal pluralism was the basic pattern of society. The most populous tribe provided the ruling family. Today tribes as a whole are under the Abu Dhabi sheikh.[10] Traditionally tribesmen were loyal to the family first, then the tribe and finally to the state.

The two major tribal groups of the United Arab Emirates are the Quasim and the Bani Yas, which enjoy immense power in UAE society. Abu Dhabi and Dubai rulers mostly belong to this Bani Yas tribe. The Quasim tribe was engaged in land and sea trade, exercised immense control over two areas such as Ras al Khaimah and Sharjah. From the eighteenth century, members of this tribe have dominated the coastal areas of these two emirates. The other tribal group, the Bani Yas, which was primarily pastoral and agricultural, settled down in Abu Dhabi and Dubai. According to tradition, Abu Dhabi has usually been ruled by a member of the Al Nahyan family while Dubai has been ruled by the Maktoum family. The Nahyans were primarily engaged in pearling during summer and in winter, they mainly cultivated dates in the desert areas. The members of the Maktoum family were mostly engaged in fishing.[11] Frauke Heard-Bay noted that among the people of the Gulf region, whether settled or Bedouin, the tribe is the principle building block for the structure of society.[12]

Place of Women in Traditional Society

The diversified economic activities of male members, often necessitating travel and absence, placed the women in a pivotal position. While their men pursued their callings outside the home for long periods, women had to shoulder various responsibilities which gave them a special position in society. According to Rosemarie Said Zahlan, "the mobility of Bedouin life has always been such that women have had a direct and active role to play in community affairs. After the Bedouin settled in the different coastal towns and villages of the Gulf, their women attained an even higher level of participation."[13] After marriage, women kept their father's name so that in case of divorce they could come back to their father's home. The norm was that after marriage the bride moved to the husband's family and stayed in separate accommodation arranged for them. According to Frauke, "because her own family is losing a worker, the groom must give compensation to the family in money or kind. At the time of the marriage contract, he also has to give the bride the means to support herself in case he was to divorce her later. This "mahr" remains her own property and is managed separately from the rest of the household."[14]

Traditional Economic Structure

Due to the shortage of arable land, most tribes used to lead a nomadic life. They used to move with their camel and goats across the desert in search of new pastures. But all the tribesmen were not nomadic, the majority of them were settled. The "versatile tribesmen" used to spent the winter with the cattle in the desert and during summer they came near the coast for fishing. Traditional occupations include camel breeding, pearling, farming, fishing and sail making.[15] Due to the harsh climate in this region agriculture was limited, and only one economically significant tree, the date palm (*Phoenix dactylifera*) grew in the desert. Thus date farming provided a limited source of income. Farmer used to irrigate their land with underground water through *falages*.[16] This *falag* system comprised subterranean stone tunnels that were designed to bring water down to the level of the towns from the high water tables of the nearby mountains. When the tunnels reached the agricultural gardens, they became surface channels, allowing the water to be regulated and redirected to whenever it was most needed.[17]

Other than this, the pearling industry and boatbuilding provided better economic opportunities for the people of this region. Before the discovery of oil, pearling was this region's major economic activity. The main reason for early population increases in Abu Dhabi was the attraction of that timeless item of adornment that is the *lulu* locally called *qamashah*, the pearl. The importance of the pearling industry can be expressed by citing the number of boats and the number of people engaged in this industry. As stated by Heard-Bay, "By the turn of the twentieth century about 1200 boats were based in ports on the Trucial Coast, manned by 22,000 men, mostly tribesmen, but with extra hands brought in from Baluchistan and elsewhere to augment the workforce."[18] This industry played a major role in transforming the traditional economy of tribal people into a modern market. Many families linked with this industry decided to settle down permanently in the coastal areas such as Abu Dhabi, Sharjah and Dubai, thus laying the foundation, as we have seen, for later waves of immigration.[19] In 1890 the pearling industry was at its peak, attracting various wealthy merchants from Bombay and East Africa during the season. These merchants used to buy the best specimen of pearls to sell to foreign clients. According to S.B. Miles, the town of Abu Dhabi had "several Hindoo traders or Banians" who resided there and handled the "bulk of the trade of the port" in the nineteenth century. Miles further stated that Debaye (Dubai) had a population of nearly 12,000 to 14,000. The trade was practically all in the hands of Banias whose strong business capacity gave them a leading position.[20]

The reasons behind the pearl boom can be better understood if we consider Lorimer's report on it. "In one year (1896-1897) pearls valued in excess of 100 lakhs were exported (approximately three quarters of a million pounds sterling), this compared with just ten lakhs per year in the 1870s."[21] Many merchants profiting from this boom began to settle down near the growing ports. During the eighteenth and nineteenth centuries, the pearl markets developed rapidly in India. As a result of growing economic opportunities, some tribes became specialized in one occupation, settled in a particular location associated with it and started leading sedentary lives.

Social Change

With the growth of the pearling industry, other ancillary economic activities started in this region. Some of these activities were small cottage industries, for example pottery, woodwork and metalwork. Pearling also encouraged the local boatbuilding industry.

With the improvement of economic conditions, demand for luxury items emerged, fuelling occupations such as tailoring and weaving.[22] Individual entrepreneurs grabbed this opening. Some of the merchants who were involved in the pearling industry or who used to provide consumer goods to the people of the UAE were able to accumulate large amount of money. Hindu merchants used to come from Bombay seasonally to Dubai. The Bania merchants from India and specially from Bombay and the Arabian Gulf provided a huge amount of finance to the pearl industry .Three reasons can be cited to show why Indian merchants were able to dominate the pearl market:

a) Their partnership with British entrepreneurs had already provided them with a capital base to invest.
b) As British subjects these merchants used to enjoy special protection from Britain.
c) Muslims were forbidden by Islamic law from charging interest on money lent.[23]

During the 1930s, due to worldwide depression and the introduction of cultured Japanese pearls in the market, this pearling industry and other coastal activities started to decline.[24] The decline in investment and profits meant the traditional diving communities began to suffer a lot of hardship. Historically, due to the scarcity of other natural resources, UAE had come to depend on a single commodity for export, and this now brought the nation face to face with disaster. Consequently UAE has remained wary of relying on a single commodity to bolster the economy and has been careful to foster other industries as well. This lesson from the past has guided its industrial policy in the post-oil era.

An important aspect of the Gulf pearling economy is that it brought the capitalist mode of production to the Emirates which had till then been absent in this area. A new local entrepreneur class began to emerge from the upper strata of the old desert hierarchy who had always been at the helm of society and now grew rich. Initially in the pearling industry there was no separation between the capitalist and the labourer: the pearl fisher owned his own boat and the whole family constituted the labour force. Later, the ownership of pearling boats diverged from the engagement in the actual diving process which is hazardous and highly skilled, leading to social divisions between boat-owners and employee divers. In the previous era a communal system had been prevalent in which the crew functioned as a mini tribe jointly owning the means of production and the profits were distributed among them according to the nature of the work.[25] While the demise in tribal solidarity brought by the capitalist mode of production might be seen as a disadvantage, on the plus side, as a result of the inflow of capital, greater trade relations developed between the Gulf and other Asian economies, especially India.

Trading had always been a characteristic occupation of the people of the Emirates. Overseas and regional trading was another means of livelihood. The lower Gulf had always been associated with the slave trade and the gold trade. Before exploration for oil, the economy was dependent on the gold trade. It is believed that one tenth of all the non-Communist world's gold passed through the various ports of this region.[26]

In short, UAE's traditional activities were based on the scarce geographical resources of the deserts. Though small scale agricultural activities were prevalent in the oasis and mountain areas, most of the people derived their living from animal husbandry, caravan trading, hunting and pearling. Pearling played a key role in the life of the people because it brought various other activities to the coast and provided a surplus on which other, more consumer-oriented occupations could subsist.

Thus we see the people of the UAE possessed extraordinary skills to survive in their harsh arid climate. Their past confidence has given them the courage to face present and future threats and challenges.

Traditional Social Structure

Society was based on tribal structure with strong bonds of consanguinity. From the distant past, class distinctions within tribes were prevalent among the nomadic people. Social stratification was based on the ownership of land in the oasis. Bedouins enjoyed higher position in the social structure. The nomads were engaged in hunting and animal husbandry. Animal husbandry has two components: sheep herding and camel herding. The camel herding tribe (*sharif*) enjoyed higher status than the sheep herding group.[27]

Changes in Traditional Society

Traditional society first underwent changes during the pearling boom. Due to urbanization, many tribes started to flock around the coasts. Semi-nomadic *bedu* could earn more money compared to other tribes because they were engaged in *ikhluw* cooperatives. They used to invest their surplus funds in the pearling industry and as a result they could transform their traditional class into a new entrepreneurial class.[28] This newly emerged class used to exercise greater political power. They used to finance various local projects and local wars.[29] A new stratification of society evolved. This new entrepreneurial class used to spend less time at the traditional property which was near oases. Due to improved economic conditions these absentee landlords used to appoint desert tribesmen to take care of their properties such as date gardens. Sometimes shortages of labourers were compensated by importing slaves. These slaves used to work as domestic servants and sometimes as divers.[30]

The aristocratic class of this society considered activities such as the dhow trade, pearling and fishing the most honourable occupations. The opportunities in other economic areas such as textiles, banking and retail trading were taken up by Hindu and Khoja groups from India.[31] According to Lorimer, during this period only ten out of seventy shops in Abu Dhabi Souk were owned by Arabs while the rest belonged to Indian merchants. The number of Indian traders in the Trucial state in the beginning of the twentieth century is represented in Table 2.1 and Table 2.2.[32]

Table 2.1: The Muslim sectors in the Trucial States in the beginning of the twentieth century

Trucial States	*Muslim*
Abu Dhabi	0
Dubai	23
Umm al Qawain	0
Ras al Khaimah	33
Sharjah	158
Total	**214**

Source: Adapted from Lorimer, Gazetteer of the Persian Gulf, vol. 1: part 2, 2379–84.

Table 2.2: The Hindu sectors in the Trucial States in the beginning of the twentieth century

Ports	*Number of Souls*	*Remarks*
Abu Dhabi	65	Includes some women and children
Dubai	67	Exclusive of about twenty visitors in the pearling season
Umm al Qwain	11	Includes women and children
Ras al Khaimah	0	
Sharjah	51	Includes some women and children
Total	**194**	

Source: Same as Table 1.

Thus we see a new socio-economic group emerging on the Trucial Coast. Indians due to their skills and other qualities were accepted and welcomed by this society. After the decline of Lingah in 1902 (see chapter 3), the number of Indians started to increase in the Trucial States especially in Dubai, as Dubai was a free port.[33] During the 1980s about 3000 Indian merchant families resided in Dubai alone. Hindu Gujaratis dominated the gold market whereas Sindhis dominated the textile trade.[34]

UAE under European Power

The importance of the past is paramount as it helps to understand the present. Therefore it is necessary to have a brief snapshot of the period when the Gulf came directly under the attention of the European powers. In the early 1500s the presence of the Portuguese marked the first European entry in this region. During the first phase of their presence, they were able to consolidate their position by use of arms. They started to build their Forts in various places. The next stage of their presence was characterized by the introduction of various trade regulations to maximize their profit. This resulted in changes in the trade pattern and their monopolization of the Indian Ocean trade.[35] The intention of the Portuguese was to monopolize the trade route between East Asia and Europe by outflanking the traditional route. The Europeans preferred the maritime route around the Cape of Good Hope which had been discovered by Portuguese navigators towards the end of the fifteenth century.[36] Gradually they established their position at various places like Khor Fakkan and Ras al Khaimah. The third phase is the stage of their decline. During the eighteenth century this Portuguese monopoly was challenged by Dutch, French and British traders. The Portuguese could not compete with the superior naval forces of the other European nations and they lost their hold. Portuguese occupation in this region had minimum impact on the regional structure.

British and Dutch Presence

The British, French and Dutch competed against each other for mercantile interests. The relationship between the Dutch and the British was cordial when their interests coincided so as to thwart Portugal's attempt to re-establish its position in the Gulf. The supremacy of the Dutch was later on challenged by Britain and Britain was able to wipe away the Dutch influence permanently from the Gulf. After the formation of the French East India Company in 1664, France entered the Gulf market but could not establish her foothold in this area. As a result Britain exercised her influence as the sole unchallenged foreign power in this region.

Britain had to face other contenders for trade. The most important threat to British interests came from the Quasimi tribes of Ras al Khaimah and Sharjah. The Quasimis started to establish themselves as traders and seafarers. During the early nineteenth century they were able to consolidate their position along the Gulf coast. But ultimately a British-Omani joint force was able to neutralize the naval power of the Quasim tribes. Thus Britain established her lasting influence in the Gulf. At the beginning of 1820 a peace treaty was signed between six sheikhs (except Fujairah) and the British government. The main purpose of the treaty was to stop piracy along the Gulf coast, which was known then as the Trucial Coast. Thus Britain established a form of political control in the external affairs of the Gulf.[37]

India had a strong link with the Gulf from time immemorial.[38] Indian presence in the gulf will be discussed in detail in a later chapter. The British withdrawal from India in 1947 did not reduce British interest or influence in the Trucial States. British interest was associated with various factors. Firstly, Gulf oil was essential to Britain as a source of energy. Secondly, the Gulf was an important stop for international air and sea communication. Nevertheless, in 1968 Britain made a ground-breaking declaration to withdraw from the Gulf. In 1971 a new nation was born, and the UAE became independent on December 2, 1971.[39]

The presence of Britain in the Gulf helped Indians to gain a new foothold in this area. The communication between Britain and the Indian empire played an important role in the area of trade relations between India and the UAE. Towards the end of the nineteenth century, individual entrepreneurs from India started to exercise their control in various sectors. With the increase in demand for consumer goods from India, Indian entrepreneurs started their investment in this region. This study will expand this aspect in detail in a later chapter.

Economic Aspects of the UAE

To better understand the UAE as a Rentier State, it is necessary to have a clear idea about a rentier economy. Beblawi in his article, "The Rentier System in the Arab World" has listed a few features of a rentier state. He notes that every economy has got some form of rent.[40]

a) If any society is dominated by the situation of rent, then it can be characterized as a rentier economy.
b) A rentier economy can sustain itself without a strong domestic sector.
c) The majority of the population are engaged in the generation, distribution and utilization of the rent, rather than in an actual production process as is normally the case.

In a Rentier State, the government is the main recipient of external rent. In such an economy, as citizens are rarely engaged in production, a special type of situation and mentality arises where citizens depend heavily on the government for the allocation of revenues. According to Abdulla Abdulkhaleq, "it results in the creation of a… paternalistic social setting with an extensive welfare structure and excessive dependence on foreign labour. In addition, a political hierarchy comes into the effect and in the due course, becomes perfectly legitimate and acceptable."[41]

On the basis of the above discussion it can be established that the UAE economy is an oil rentier state as the modern economy is still heavily dependent on oil where the primary source of income is the oil sector. According to Abdullah, "during the1980s more than 90 percentage of the Gulf state's total revenue came from oil, mostly in the form of royalties and from international oil companies' leasing agreements.'[42]

In the Rentier State structure, the ruler and his family will be in the upper strata of society and foreign labour remains at the bottom. The middle strata comprises mostly local nationals. These nationals due to their citizenship rights enjoy many privileges. External rent is controlled by the government and on that basis the government of such a State exercises and enjoys enormous economic and political power. Government plays a key role in distributing wealth to the population. On the basis of the above discussion it can be concluded that UAE is an oil rentier economy.

Economic Role of the State

The economic role of the state is highly significant and powerful in the United Arab Emirates. The main recipients of the oil revenues are Abu Dhabi and Dubai. Since the ruling families practically run the government of the UAE, it may be surmised that it is the ruling families that are the main recipients of the oil revenue. ADNOC (Abu Dhabi National Oil Company) is the largest oil company, established in the year 1971 and wholly owned by the government. The ADNOC group includes seventeen companies which deal with all oil- and gas-related production functions in the Emirates. ADNOC is the eighth largest recipient of US federal contract dollars, receiving a total of $918,256,500 in 2008 alone. Abu Dhabi is the oil producer in the UAE controlling more than 85 percent of the UAE's total oil output capacity and over 90% of its crude reserve. The ADNOC group is controlled and supervised by the Supreme Petroleum Council (SPC) which formulates petroleum policy. The SPC is chaired by His Highness Sheikh Khalifa Bin Zayed Al-Nahyan, the present President of the UAE and ruler of Abu Dhabi. Today ADNOC has placed itself in the top 10 oil and gas companies in the world, and manages and oversees oil production of 2.7 million barrel a day.[43]

In addition to ADNOC's fifty percent share of the total oil production, the government receives revenue from all international oil companies who enter into agreements with the government. In Dubai, the main operators are the government-owned Dubai Petroleum Company and Dubai Natural Gas Company.

Background of the UAE Federation

On January 16, 1968, the British Government announced its decision to withdraw from the Gulf region. The sudden declaration of withdrawal put this region into an uncomfortable situation. As appropriate territorial boundaries were not drawn between states, the rulers were not in a position to solve unresolved territorial disputes. Two other factors also contributed to the formation of the federation. The sudden growth in oil revenue coupled with new ideological trends sweeping this region brought the leaders closer to avoid subversion. These three factors worked in cementing the bond between the smaller states to form one super-state.[44]

To work towards the formation of the federation, the initial steps were taken by Dubai and Abu Dhabi. Open invitations were extended to other rulers to join. Initially Bahrain and Qatar agreed to join, but later on both Qatar and Bahrain declared their own independence and declined to be a part of the UAE federation. The differences in the sizes of the territories, population structure, education level and economic development of the member-states created hindrances in the institution making process.[45] On December 2, 1971, six emirates including Abu Dhabi, Dubai, Sharjah, Ajman and Fujairah agreed to adopt the provisional constitution. Ras al Khaimah joined the federation in February 1972.[46]

Constitution of the UAE

The Constitution of the UAE came into operation on December 2, 1971. The provisional Constitution of the UAE was meant to be in operation for five years only but the permanent Constitution came into force only in 1996. During 1971-1996, the provisional constitution was renewed every five years. Abu Dhabi was accepted as the capital of the UAE by seven emirates.[47]

Union Authorities: According to Article 45 of the Constitution,[48] the Union authorities shall consist of:

a) The supreme council of the Union.
b) The President of the Union and his Deputy.
c) The Council of Ministers of the Union.
d) The National Assembly of the Union.
e) The Judiciary of the Union.

Each emirate enjoys its own political and judicial power. According to article 120 of the UAE Constitution, the Federal government exercises control over foreign affairs, defence and the armed forces, health, education, postal and telegraph services and electricity services. Individual emirates are responsible for "development in civil aviation, oil, internal security, finance and investment and economic policy."[49]

Supreme Council: The supreme council is the highest federal authority, according to Article 46, composed of the rulers of the seven emirates. According to article 47, the supreme council can exercise the following powers:[50]

a) To formulate the general policy in all matters vested in the Union by the Constitution in order to fulfil the goals of the union and promote the common interest of all the seven emirates.
b) To sanction different union laws before final promulgation, which includes the final accounts and the laws pertaining to the Annual General Budget.
c) To ratify treaties and international agreements.
d) To approve the appointment of the Chairman of the Council of Ministers of the Union, or to accept his or her resignation etc.
e) To approve the appointment of the president and judges of the supreme court of the Union.
f) To exercise supreme control over Union affairs.
g) To ratify federal laws, although the president has the right to amend them.

The President of the UAE is the head of the state who is elected by, and from, the supreme council of the rulers. The President and the

Vice President are elected for renewable five year terms. The head of the state is the Commander-in-Chief of the armed forces. From the beginning the President has been elected from Abu Dhabi whereas the Vice Presidency and Prime Ministerial positions are held by the rulers of Dubai. There is less chance of change in this tradition.[51]

Council of Ministers: According to Article 55, the Council of Ministers of the Union is composed of the Prime Minister, his Deputy Minister and a number of Ministers. The Council of Ministers introduces legislation which is ratified by the Supreme Council. In 1971, six ministerial departments were given to Abu Dhabi including foreign affairs, the interior and information. Three ministries were given to Dubai and Sharjah dealing with defence, finance, economy and commerce, and two ministries were given to Fujairah and Ras Al Khaimah. One each was provided to Ajman and Umm al Quwain. During March 1997, the first cabinet reshuffle was made in seven years. The most striking thing about this is the how the ruler of Dubai, Sheikh Maktoum, brought many competent young administrators into government departments.[52]

Federal National Council (Legislature): Article 68 of the UAE Constitution states that the national assembly of the Union shall be composed of forty members. Seats shall be distributed to members of the Emirates as follows: Abu Dhabi, 8 seats; Dubai, 8 seats; Sharjah, 6 seats; Ras Al Khaimah, 6 seats; Ajman, 4 seats; Umm Al Quwain, 4 seats and Fujairah, 4 seats. Representation in the FNC is based on the population of each emirate. The members are to represent the country as a whole and not their individual emirates (Article 77). They play only a consultative role. For the first time, a small section of UAE nationals enjoyed their right to vote by electing 20 members to the Federal National Council. Though the majority of them could not exercise their voting rights, most of the UAE nationals believe that the concept of democracy is not new to them. They have been practicing democracy in the past through the tribal custom of *majlis* or assembly where the people's voice reaches the decision-maker.[53]

Judiciary of the UAE: Articles 94 to 109 of the UAE Constitution deal with the judicial power.[54] According to article 95, "The Union shall have a Union Supreme Court and Union Primary Tribunals." The Federal or Union Supreme Court is composed of a president and not more than 5 judges. They are to be appointed by decrees promulgated by the President of the Union (article 96). The Supreme Court is entrusted with the following functions:

First, it may adjudicate disputes between member emirates of the Union, or one or more emirates and the federal government, "Whenever such disputes are submitted to the court on the request of the any of the interested parties."(article 99, clause 1)

Second, it enjoys the power to judge the constitutionality of the Federal Laws (article 99)

Third, it has the power to interpret the provisions of the Constitution upon a request received from any Federal or emirate government. (article 99, clause 2)

Fourth, the interpretation and judgement of the Union Supreme Court is final and binding upon all the parties. (article 101)

The principle features of the UAE Constitution are as follows:

a) It is a written constitution.
b) It is a rigid constitution.
c) It centralizes authority in the President of the federation and the Federal Supreme Council.
d) The Islamic *shariah* shall be a main source of legislation. Article 7 of the UAE Constitution established the role of Islamic *shariah* law in the legal system, stating, "Islam is the official religion of the federation. The Islamic *shariah* shall be a main source of legislation in the federation..." as UAE is an Islamic society in which the ruler and the people believe Islamic law to be the supreme law.[55]

As discussed earlier, tribe and family play a key role in the political organization of the UAE. Rulers are chosen from prominent sheikh families who are believed to be more competent and qualified than others. Normally the head of the state before his death will recommend the name of his son or another competent member of the family whom he finds appropriate for the position of his successor. The family also has the absolute power to replace a ruler who does not abide by the policies and norms of the families. According to Herb, the "UAE is a dynastic monarchy."[56] According to Hudson, "The sheikh of a tribe leads by virtue of his personal qualities as recognised by the Council of Elders—the heads of the main families."[57]

The UAE is formed by seven emirates, Abu Dhabi, Dubai, Sharjah, Ajman, Umm Al Quwain, Ras Al Khaimah and Fujairah. Each emirate's political and financial position is reflected by the allocation of its position in the federal system. Abu Dhabi is the main oil producer among the seven: its ruler is the President of the UAE. Dubai is the main commercial centre of the UAE and it also has a major share in oil production: the ruler of Dubai is the Vice President and Prime Minister of the UAE. Each emirate enjoys extensive autonomy .The most important aspect of the UAE Federation is that a major portion of each emirate's revenue should be allocated to the UAE's central budget.

In the UAE there are no political parties. The rulers enjoy their powers on the basis of their legitimacy in the system of tribal consensus. In spite of rapid modernisation and influx of foreign workers, UAE still maintains its traditional political system.

Location, Geography and Society

The United Arab Emirates is located north of the equator between latitude 22 and 26.5 north and longitude 51 and 56.25 east. The total area is approximately 84,650 square kilometres. It is bounded by the Arabian Sea to the south and west and to the North West, the kingdoms of Saudi Arabia and Qatar. The sultanate of Oman borders it to the east. Its coastline of 644 kilometres on the Arabian Sea is shared by the seven emirates of the UAE.

***Climate*:** The UAE's climate is extremely hot and humid in summer. From May to October the temperature may range between 38 degrees centigrade to 50 degrees centigrade in the middle of the day and during the night it can drop to 20 degrees centigrade. In winter average temperature is usually around 15.5 degrees centigrade. Rain is infrequent and irregular and falls mainly between November and April. As in all desert environments, sandstorms are an important feature of the climate.

Population: Though the climate of the UAE is mainly inhospitable, due to rapid growth and modernization, the population of the UAE has increased. According to the latest census, the total population is 4,104,695. Nationals comprise 21.9% and the rest are foreigners. The majority of the UAE population is predominantly urban, and mostly they reside in Dubai, Abu Dhabi and Sharjah. Expatriates are in a majority.[58]

Resources: Wells and underground canals from the mountains are the main natural source of water of the United Arab Emirates. The major resource of the UAE is petroleum. Other than that it has poor agricultural and mineral resources.

Social Structure: Due to the oil boom there is a constant influx of foreigners. These immigrants and expatriate workers do not enjoy any political rights. Under pressure from social change and rampant migration the ancient nomadic tribes are vanishing.

Religion: Most of the citizens of the United Arab Emirates are Sunni Muslims. The foreign population includes Shia and Sunni Muslims, Hindus and Christians. The degree of religious freedom varies from one emirate to another. Non-Muslims enjoy more religious freedom in the UAE compared to Saudi Arabia and Qatar, though numbers of Muslims are higher in the UAE than Saudi Arabia and Qatar. Non-Muslims are given the right to worship but not to proselytize. Hindus have constructed temples in Dubai. There are many Christian churches in Dubai and Abu Dhabi.[59]

Political Aspects: Democracy here is perhaps not as prevalent as in some other countries, however, limited franchise exits. Only a small section of the national population enjoys the right to vote by electing twenty members of Federal National Council, while the majority of them cannot exercise their voting rights. Most UAE nationals believe that their tribal life was founded on the concept of democracy. The tribal custom of assembly or *majlis* allowed the ordinary people to air their grievances and make applications to the tribal decision maker. A unique *majlis* tradition is still prevalent in this area where the prominent members of the UAE, tribal leaders and rulers meet guests to hear the problems of the common people. The rulers of UAE are always in close touch with their subjects. Though the Western type of democracy is not prevalent in this region, the *majlis* offers an alternative that does not go against tribal values. The advent of modern life has not changed their attitude.

Conclusion

Prior to December 1971 the seven emirates were economically separate under British rule. They were underdeveloped and socially backward. Health, education and housing facilities were not up to the mark. By contrast at present the scenario in the UAE is totally different. As far as living standards are concerned, the country has been able to place itself in the company of high income nations. The credit goes to enlightened leaders whose successful policies and programmes have made the UAE a unique place. The transition process towards modernity was very smooth, and in this the political stability of the UAE has also contributed to its success.

ENDNOTES

1. Ibrahim Al-Abed and Peter Hellyer, eds, *United Arab Emirates* (Abu Dhabi: Trident Press and Ministry of Information and Culture, 1997), 32.
2. Frauke Heard-Bay, ed., *From Trucial States to United Arab Emirates: A Society in Transition* (Singapore: Longman, 1982), 21.
3. Ministry of Information and Culture, UAE, *The United Arab Emirates: An Ancient People and a Young Country* (Abu Dhabi: Ministry of Information and Culture, 1992), 13.
4. Heard-Bay, *From Trucial States*, 2.
5. J.G. Lorimer, cited in Frauke Heard-Bay, "The Tribal Society of the UAE and its Traditional Economy," in *Perspectives on the United Arab Emirates*, eds. Edmund Ghareeb and Ibrahim-Al-Abed (London: Trident Press, 1997), 256.
6. Rosemarie Said Zahlan, *The Origins of United Arab Emirates: Political and Social History of the Trucial States* (London: Macmillan, 1978), 4.
7. Heard-Bay, *From Trucial States*, 261.
8. Edward Henderson, *This Strange Eventful History: Memories of Earlier Days in the United Arab Emirates and the Sultanate of Oman* (Dubai: Motivate Publishing, 1988), 34.
9. Ibid., 40.
10. Ibid., 39-41.
11. Heard-Bay, *From Trucial States*, 32.
12. Heard-Bay, "Tribal Society," 257.
13. Rosemarie Said Zahlan, *The Making of the Modern Gulf States: Kuwait, Bahrain, Qatar, the United Arab Emirates and Oman* (London: Ithaca, 1998), 5.
14. Heard-Bay, "Tribal Society," 255.
15. Heard-Bay, *From Trucial States*, 24-5.
16. Aqil Kasim, *The United Arab Emirates, A.D. 600 to the Present: A Socio-Discursive Transformation in the Arabian Gulf* (Dubai: Gulf Book Centre, 2000), 185.
17. J.G. Lorimer, *Gazetteer of the Persian Gulf, Oman and Central Arabia*, vol. 1: part 2 (Calcutta: Government Press, 1970), 2379–84.
18. Heard-Bay, "Tribal Society," 262.
19. Ibid.
20. S.B. Miles, *The Countries and Tribes of the Persian Gulf* (London: Frank Cass, 1966), 441.
21. Christopher M. Davidson, *The United Arab Emirates: A Study in Survival* (Boulder: Lynne Rienner, 2005), 6.
22. Heard-Bay, *From Trucial States*, 195.
23. Muhammad Morsy Abdullah, *United Arab Emirates: A Modern History* (London and New York: Croom Helm and Barnes and Noble, 1978), 105.

24. Kevin G. Fenelon, *The United Arab Emirates: An Economic and Social Survey* (London: Longman, 1973), 56.
25. Davidson, *Study in Survival*, 8.
26. Ibid., 9.
27. Ibid., 6.
28. Heard-Bay, "Tribal Society," 263.
29. Abdullah, *Modern History*, 104.
30. Heard-Bay, *From Trucial States*, 200.
31. Abdullah, *Modern History*, 104–05.
32. Adapted from Lorimer, *Gazetteer of the Persian Gulf*, vol. 1: part 2, 2379–84.
33. Fatma Al-Sayegh, "Merchants' Role in a Changing Society: The Case of Dubai, 1900-90," *Middle Eastern Studies* 34, no. 1 (January 1998): 87–102.
34. Myron Weiner, "International Migration and Development: Indians in the Persian Gulf," in *Indian Diaspora in West Asia,* ed. Prakash C. Jain (New Delhi: Manohar, 2007), 144.
35. Fenelon, Economic and Social Survey, 9.
36. Zahlan, *Modern Gulf States*, 10.
37. *Fenelon,* Economic and Social Survey, 9.
38. Zahlan, *Modern Gulf States*, 20.
39. *Economist*, "Country Profile 2000: United Arab Emirates," *Economist Intelligence Unit* (2000): 4, http:// www.eiu.com (accessed July 13, 2010).
40. Hazem Beblawi, "The Rentier State in the Arab World," in *The Arab State*, ed. G. Luciani (London: Routledge, 1990), 87–9.
41. Abdulkhaleq Abdulla, *The Arab Gulf States: Old Approaches and New Realities; The Emirates Occasional Papers*, no. 40 (Abu Dhabi: The Emirates Centre for Strategic Studies and Research, 2000), 12.
42. *Ibid.*, 12–3.
43. Source: Abu Dhabi National Oil Company (ADNOC), http:// www.adnoc.ae/content.aspx?mid=22 (accessed November 11, 2010).
44. Frauke Heard-Bay, *The United Arab Emirates, A Quarter Century of Federation in Middle East Dilemma: The Politics and Economics of Arab Integration* (New York: Columbia University Press, 1999), 31.
45. *Ibid.*, 129.
46. *Ibid.*, 134.
47. UAE Constitution, art. 2.
48. UAE Constitution, "Union Authorities," part 4, art. 45.
49. "Country Profile 2000," *Economist Intelligence Unit*, 6–8.
50. UAE Constitution, "Union Authorities," part 4: chap. 1, arts. 46–7.
51. Country Profile 2000, *Economist Intelligence Unit*, 6.

52. *Ibid.*, 7.
53. *Ibid.*, 7.
54. UAE Constitution, "Judiciary in the Union and the Emirates," part 4: chap. 5, art. 94–109.
55. Saeed M.A.O. Al-Ghufli, *Judicial Review of the Constitutionality in the United Arab Emirates: A Comparative Interaction* (Dubai: Dubai Police Academy, 2002–03), 72–3.
56. Michael Herb, *All in the Family: Absolutism, Revolution and Democracy in the Middle Eastern Monarchies*, (New York: Suny Press, 1999).
57. Michael C. Hudson, *Arab Politics: The Search for Legitimacy*, (New Haven: Yale University Press, 1977), 89.
58. *Source*: http://www.infoplease.com/ipa/A0108074.html (accessed November 12, 2010).
59. Federal Research Division, Library of Congress, *United Arab Emirates: A Country Study*, (Washington DC: Federal Research Division, Library of Congress, 2005), 81.

3

Indo-UAE Bilateral Commercial Relations

India and the seven emirates which now form the United Arab Emirates have had social and mercantile contact since the third century BCE.[1] India's interaction with this region was mainly based on commerce. People-to-people contact and barter trade between the Indic and the present-day UAE regions helped them develop a comprehensive and diversified relationship. This long-term partnership was based on shared geopolitical and historical realities.

The strong commercial relationship between the Indic and Arab regions resulted in some cultural exchanges as well. The relationship deepened further during the rise of Islam. The period between the seventh and the tenth century BCE is considered the golden age of Indo-Arab trade relations.[2] Long-term cultural contact, however, started around the middle of the eighth century BCE and has since been a reciprocal exchange.

Export-Import Items between India and the UAE

The teak wood that was used for boat-building and house-building in the Arabic region was exported by India. The most sought-after item, however, was the Indian sword which was named *Al Muhanned* by the Arabs, favoured for its sharpness and suppleness. Besides swords, raw iron was also imported in large quantities from India. Silver and other metals, diamonds and crystals, pearls from Subara (Sopra, near Bombay) were among the other items imported from India. Another item favoured by the Arabs was the horn of the rhinoceros which was used to manufacture ornaments and sold as high-priced luxury items. Diamonds from Kashmir and gold from Kamrupa were among other high-priced Arab imports from India.

The transaction between the Malabar coast of India and the Gulf coast largely centred around spices—pepper, cardamom and cinnamon. Sandalwood, aloe-wood and perfumes were also exported. Among fruits, mangoes, jackfruits, lemons, citrons and coconuts were exported from India to the Arabs. Elephants, peacocks, fine muslin cotton cloths, indigo and dyes were exported too. Among the items imported by India were frankincense, ivory/tusks, horses, gold, pearls, dates, and other finished goods.

According to S. Maqbul Ahmad, "On the basis of the accounts of the Arab writers of this period, it may be summarised that the total balance of trade must have been favourable to India. Firstly, gold was used by Indian merchants as means of exchange. Secondly, the volume of India's exports seems to have far exceeded that of the Arab countries to India. Lastly, the goods exported from India were costlier than those imported by India".[3]

That India's linkage with the UAE and other Arab states pre-dates the oil era is clear. The emergence of the UAE as a federation has further solidified this relationship, and both sides are striving to bolster the relationship for mutual benefit. The level of interaction between the two regions has gained strength with the rise of the UAE as important exporter of oil and gas to the Indian market. Indo-UAE trade, valued at $180 million per annum in the 1970s, was valued at $29,023.68 million for the financial year 2007–08.[4] After Singapore and Hong Kong, UAE has emerged as the third major re-export centre in the world. The emergence of UAE as a re-export centre has helped the growth of bilateral relations between India and the UAE.

India's exports to the UAE, today, are well diversified with a larger basket. Major items exported to the UAE are RMG cotton including accessories, gems and jewellery, manmade yarn, fabrics, and metal. In return, UAE exports petroleum products, precious and semi-precious metals, and stones sulphur and pearls— local goods that are in abundance in this region.

India-UAE Energy Cooperation

India has been actively purchasing energy from the major companies in the UAE such as ADNOC (Abu Dhabi National Oil Company). Major Indian companies like Punj Lloyd have established and completed major projects in the oil and gas sectors in the UAE. Both countries are interested in future sustainability of energy resources and the means to expand energy capacities. This has been demonstrated with a research agreement signed between Rajendra K. Pachauri, Director General of TERI (The Energy and Research

Institute), India, and the Higher College of Technology, UAE, to examine technologies that will assist in expanding energy resources for the future. The potential for energy-partnership between the two countries lies in the fact that UAE has a high hydrocarbon reserve and India is a major consumer of hydrocarbons. There also lies the potential for partnership in education and research in this field as India has a high level of expertise in the sector of renewable energy.

Major Events, Conferences and Exchange Visits

India Trade Promotion Organisation team's visit to the UAE: A two-member team, comprising the Executive Director and the General Manager of ITPO, met with H.E. Mohammed Rashed Al Hameli, Director General of Abu Dhabi Chamber of Commerce and Industry (ADCCI) and engaged in discussions about trade and commerce, and bilateral ties between the two nations.

Khalifa International Date Palm Awards: Atul Limited, a leading chemical company in India with a strong focus on environmental care, was awarded the prestigious award worth 2 million Dirhams in recognition of its extensive work in promoting the date palm in India.

International Defense Exhibition (IDEX 2009): The ninth edition of the IDEX witnessed major participation from Indian exhibitors such as the Ordinance Factory Board (Kolkata), and a demonstration of the Hydrographic Survey Vessel from the Indian Navy.

India-UAE Trade Policy Forum: The UAE forum, led by the Minister of Economy, discussed the need to establish more branches of Indian banks in the UAE and decrease existing bans imposed on items of import such as poultry products.

Third India-GCC Industrial Conference: The conference that was held in Mumbai focussed on the potential for mutual investments between India and the Gulf countries.

Joint Commission: A joint commission between India and the UAE was set up in 1975 that has since been organizing annual meetings and maintaining a forum to discuss issues in promoting bilateral cooperation in trade, investment, education, culture, health, science and technology, as well as controlling crime and terrorism.

Joint Business Council: A joint business council was set up in Mumbai between the Chambers of Commerce of both countries to pursue issues pertaining to areas of interest between the two countries.

Bilateral Agreements: Bilateral agreements between the two countries hold the key to forming a smoothly functioning working relationship. In the economic field these include:

- Agreement of Avoidance of Double Taxation (April, 1992).
- Civil Aviation Agreement (1989).
- Framework Agreement for developing industrial relations (March, 2007).
- Memorandum of Understanding for technical cooperation, signed between the Bureau of Indian Standards and the Emirates Authority for Standardisation and Metrology.
- Memorandum of Understanding for technical cooperation in accreditation activities between the National Accreditation Board for Testing and Calibration Laboratories and the Emirates Authority for Standardisation and Metrology.
- Memorandum of Understanding between the Securities and Exchange Board of India and the Emirates Securities and Commodities Authority for assistance and mutual cooperation in exchange of information.

Apart from these public ventures, there are a range of private bilateral agreements that include:

- A fifty-fifty joint venture agreement between Nakheel, Dubai's largest property developer and the DLF Group, one of the leading real estate companies in India.
- A technology solutions corporation between Dubai Islamic Bank, Dubai World and Wipro Technologies.
- The setting up of a Videocon manufacturing plant in Dubai.
- The setting up of a manufacturing unit in Dubai for Ashok Leyland, the Hinduja Group's flagship firm. The Hinduja group also has plans to launch its first hospital in Dubai within a few years' time.
- Nakheel and Limitless, two Dubai-based real estate groups, are making major investments in India, near New Delhi and Mumbai.

Civil Aviation Talks: Talks are in progress to enable cross-border aviation operations of all national flight leagues in the UAE and in India.

Free Trade Agreement: India and GCC have signed a Framework Agreement on Economic Cooperation (August 2004) whereby the growing importance of economic and commercial relations between

India and GCC countries has been acknowledged and has facilitated the entering into a Free Trade Agreement.

NRI Remittances: The annual remittances made by the large Indian expat community in the UAE are estimated to be over $2 billion per annum.

Banking: Indian banks like the Bank of Baroda have had major operating branches in the UAE since 1974, and UAE-based banks such as the Abu Dhabi Commercial Bank and the Mashreq Bank have 3 branches among themselves in India.

Important Indian personalities who have visited the UAE: Among the important Indian figures who have visited the UAE are the Indian President, Pratibha Patil. While on her visit, she stated in an interview to the *Gulf News*: "Trade and investment will be the cornerstone of partnership in the evolving global scenario.... Whilst trade has been the bedrock of our economic partnership, strengthening the flow of Foreign Direct Investment between the two countries can be a pillar of our relationship." [5]

Shaikha Lubna Al-Qasimi, the UAE Minister of Foreign Trade, who was also present in the meetings held with Ms Patil, said that India-UAE trade exchange over the last decade has multiplied thirteen times with non-oil sectors slowly gaining a predominant share.

The Indian Minister for External Affairs, Pranab Mukherjee, visited the UAE in 2008 and met with H.H. General Sheikh Mohammed Bin Zayed Al Nahyan, Abu Dhabi Crown Prince, to review the progress of the JCM and cooperation in addressing the worldwide increase in food prices.

The Indian Minister for Commerce and Industry, Kamal Nath, visited in 2008, where he addressed the desire to promote mutual investments in both countries and called upon the two governments to work together to forge a new partnership.

Joint Ventures in India by UAE-based Companies

Emaar, a leading Dubai-based real estate company, has invested up to $500 million in real estate projects in India. They are also setting up satellite townships in the states of Andhra Pradesh, Punjab and Delhi. Emaar had also bagged the contract to build the $170 million Commonwealth Games Village in Delhi.

Dubai Ports World is working on container transhipment terminals at major ports in India, as well as shouldering the responsibilities for operating six major ports in India.

Smart City, a project township worth $350 million with 70 percent IT and IT enabled services, has been developed in Kochi. It is the second largest foreign direct investment in Kerala.

In May 2007, ETA Star Properties signed an MoU with the Tamil Nadu state government to set up a dedicated IT hub in the township of Kancheepuram, which is estimated to be worth $923 million.

In August 2007, the Lootah Group (a Dubai-based conglomerate), opened a wholly owned subsidiary in India, entering into two MoUs with a Hyderabad-based infrastructure company, to explore infrastructure development opportunities in India.

Joint Ventures/Contractual Participation by Indian Companies in the UAE

Dheeraj and East Coast is a joint venture between an Indian and an UAE based business groups. They are developing projects worth $0.27 billion in the Dubai Business Bay.

L&T and its Oman-based subsidiary secured five major contracts for the construction of major water supply projects and luxury condominiums in the UAE.

The Hinduja Group has signed an MoU with the Ras Al Khaimah Investment Authority to set up a bus and vehicle assembly plant for its flagship brand Ashok Leyland.

Nakheel, UAE, joined forces with the Larsen and Toubro Group, India, to build a residential project worth Rs 2 billion in Jumeirah Island, in Dubai.

Dubai Investments Company signed an agreement with SKS Ispat and Power Ltd in India to set up steel fabrication facilities worth $25 million.

Tata Realty and Infrastructure signed a fifty-fifty joint venture with Jafza International to engage in developing a network of business and logistics parks.

Conclusion

Despite the proximity and cultural and commercial ties between India and the UAE, the full potential of the business capacity between these two nations has not yet been tapped. Both India and UAE are now making an active effort to maximize this potential through revised policy formulations and strengthening the bilateral ties between them in both the public and private sectors.

Observing the valuations of the investment projects outlined above, it is quite clear that a strong and healthy working relationship between these two nations can only prove to be favourable to both.

ENDNOTES

1. Abdulla Elamadani, "India's Impact on the Gulf's Economic and Socio-Cultural Life During the British Era," in *India Diaspora in West Asia: A Reader*, ed. Prakash C. Jain, 45 (New Delhi: Manohar, 2007).
2. S. Maqbul Ahmed, *Indo-Arab Relations* (New Delhi: Indian Council for Cultural Relations, 1971).
3. *Ibid*., 87.
4. Indian Embassy in Abu Dhabi, UAE.
5. *Gulf News*, Excerpts from an interview with Pratibha Patil, November 26, 2010.

4

Indian Diaspora in the UAE

This chapter focuses on the nature of the Indian diaspora in the UAE: the migration process undergone by the Indians of this diaspora, their struggles to overcome the challenges they faced in this process, and the key role played by this "incipient" diaspora in the UAE in various fields—such as remittance, FDI, short-term capital flow and business creation—and in developing bilateral relations between India and the UAE.

The effects of globalization have been ubiquitous. Regardless of all criticism, there is no denying it. As Paola Grenier puts it: "Globalization is the growing interdependence and integration between economies and societies around the world."[1] And according to Stanley J. Tambiah, the most important feature of globalization is the "transnational movement of people" and the "intensification in the creation of diverse diasporic populations in many locations, who are engaged in complex interpersonal and intercultural relationships with both their host societies and their societies of origin."[2] We will try and analyse how centrally the Indian diaspora in the UAE is placed in this process of globalization.

There is a need to establish whether this diasporic Indian entrepreneurship in the UAE is an important part of this globalization process and to what extent they can be considered assets to both India and the UAE. The process of globalization has created a new trend in the global migration process where such diasporas are centrally located in this picture. They act as a linkage between different geographical locations. That the diasporic entrepreneurs in the UAE, particularly the Indian diasporic entrepreneurs of this region, did not receive due appreciation and must be viewed as a highly different and special group is arguable. The study will also try and analyse why the Indian diaspora of this region is more successful compared to the diasporic presence in other advanced countries, and attempt to establish how their networking and special innovation skills have placed them in this special category. In this context, it is necessary to have a clear idea about various Indian migration processes, as a brief analysis of the history of migration will help us better understand the various factors that leads to and are related to human migration, and goes on to define the diasporas as we know of them. For this purpose, this study shall briefly look into the history of Indian migrations later in this chapter. But before that the study will look into the existing definitions of the term "diaspora", and will also make an attempt to see the Indian diaspora/diasporic entrepreneurs in the UAE in this light.

Definition of Diaspora

The term "diaspora" has created many debates in recent years. According to Martin Bauman: "Within various disciplines of the humanities, 'diaspora' has become one of the most fashionable terms in the late twentieth century."[3] Historically the term diaspora "has been consistently associated with experience of displacement, dispersal and migrancy; however the concept has remained peripheral in debates in human migration and mobility until fairly recently."[4] The noun "diaspora" is derivative of a Greek composite verb "dia" and "speirein" (diaspeirein, infinitive) meaning "to scatter", to spread" or "to disperse." To Greeks the term "diaspora"—"Sperio", meaning "to sow", and the preposition "dia", meaning "to spread over"—meant migration and colonization.[5] Until 1960 it was used from the standpoint of Jewish history. In Hebrew the term is "galut", which initially referred to the scattered settlement of Jewish colonies outside of Palestine after the Babylonian exile.

During the year 1970 the term diaspora acquired a more general connotation referring to every person residing far away from their ancestral home/country.[6] In the context of the UAE, however, the term diaspora has broader semantic implications. Here the concept of diaspora has more theoretic considerations beyond a mere descriptive term. Instead of the conventional focal standpoint of forced dispersal, such as Jews, Greeks and Armenians, here it can be viewed from a more global and transnational perspective. As Judith T. Shuval rightly pointed out: "The term has acquired a broad semantic domain and now encompasses an array of groups such as political refugees, alien residents, guest workers, immigrants, expatriates, ethnic and racial minorities, as well as overseas communities."[7]

William Safron has argued that other expatriated communities such as Armenians, Chinese, Greek, Indians, Kurdish, Palestinian, and Persians could be placed within the domain of diaspora if they fulfil the following criteria:[8]

a) They or their predecessors have relocated from their location of origin to a new location.
b) They have a shared memory of their original homeland and its culture.
c) They struggle to fit in with the host community and often face various tribulations.
d) They have their original homeland as a possible venue of return should the conditions call for it.
e) Their bond with their homeland is strong and they continue to actively maintain and sustain this bond. This can be achieved by helping their community back in their homeland either financially or psychologically.
f) They try to set themselves apart in their new location by adapting their original cultural values into the culture of that place.

Cohen (1997), on the other hand, based on similar perspectives, has categorized diasporas on the basis of various diasporic experiences, as represented below:[9]

a) Victim Diaspora which includes Jews, Africans, Armenians
b) Labour Diaspora (e.g. Indian Indentured labourers)
c) Trade Diaspora (e.g. Chinese and Lebanese)
d) Imperial Diaspora (e.g. British)
e) Cultural Diaspora (e.g. Caribbean)

According to Khacahig Toololyan, "migrations have led to a proliferation of diasporas and to a redefinition of their importance and roles.... We used 'diaspora' provisionally to indicate our belief that the term that once described Jewish, Greek, and Armenian dispersion now shares meanings with a larger semantic domain that includes words like immigrant, expatriate, refugee, guest worker, exile community, overseas community, ethnic community. This is the vocabulary of transnationalism, and any of its term can usefully be considered under more than one of its rubrics."[10]

Thus we see the concept of diaspora must be understood from various perspectives. The objective of this study has been to define the Indian diaspora in the UAE from the perspective of globalization. Undeniably it can be argued that the recent flow of migration in the UAE is the result of global communication. Gabriel Sheffer concentrated his attention on the emergence of a new ethnic "incipient diaspora" and studied the conditions which supported its growth. He claims that lack of favourable economic conditions along with newfound political freedom motivated a large number of people to migrate in search of better fortunes. He also argued that "as a result of communication and transportation revolution, which has facilitated the rapid spread of news, fashions, as well as social and political trends, openness and tolerance have spread and increased. Moreover, the information about these general trends, about the specific conditions prevailing in different host countries and about the movement of large groups further influenced migration, and eventually the decision to settle in the host countries."[11] Nowadays the term diaspora is used in a broader sense. In common practice the term diaspora refers to the people who have a common ancestral homeland, who have a sense of separateness and are marginalized in the host society. The pattern of migration may be voluntary or involuntary. The focus of this study is on the role of diasporic entrepreneurs in the UAE. The term diaspora in this context will refer to the Indians who have left India in search of semi-permanent habitat with financial stability. They are a part of the globalization process and are unique in maintaining their identities and having a strong bond with their motherland.

The nature of Indian diaspora in the UAE is quite different from that of the other diasporas in the world, as their desire to settle in the UAE is limited by the legal setup of the host country such as lack of citizenship rights for foreigners, etc. However, it can be argued that in spite of various difficulties associated with their stay in this region these "greener pastures" will continue to attract many Indians to come to this region. A majority of Indians choose to live in this country for more than twenty five to thirty years by renewing their visas every three years. As this diaspora is aware of the temporary nature of their stay, they maintain closer ties with their homeland compared to the migrants in other developed countries. As pointed out earlier, more of the next generation Indian diaspora were compelled to go abroad for their higher studies but many of them came back to the UAE for better economic fortunes. The interviewees from the second generation business group showed a strong desire to continue their activities in this region.[12] But it has to be acknowledged that the openness and tolerance of the UAE has encouraged this incipient diaspora to act as a bridge between the two nations.

Various studies have been carried out but Indians in the UAE were never given proper consideration by them. There has been a component of negligence on the part of the researchers conducting various studies on the contribution of skill migration regarding the value assessment of Indian diasporic entrepreneurs in the UAE and there is a need for further studies regarding their contribution. According to Solimano, the skilled diasporic entrepreneurs are an important part of the transnational entrepreneurship. But the diaspora in the UAE, though most of them were not skilled émigrés, are also to be credited because they played an active role as global agents. Their talent for business creation, resource mobilization and other contributions to their homelands as well as host countries deserve due recognition. Solimano summarized that not only highly skilled entrepreneurs, but all "people with talent for business creation and resource mobilization rather than necessarily individuals with a high stock of formal education" are crucial to the globalization process.[13]

The contribution of the Indian diasporic entrepreneurs is immense. The illuminating examples of many such successful entrepreneurs in the UAE reflect their innovative skill. Their contributions of various kinds e.g. remittances, foreign direct investment, short-term capital flows, and business creation have tremendous economic importance and social consequences. The recipients of the Padmashree Award justified the statement that they are making history in spite of various hardships faced by them. It is expected that their spectacular achievements will draw attention from further researchers towards this regions. The following section of this study will briefly look into the history of Indian migration.

Indian Migration History

Migration is one of the oldest phenomena in both human and animal history. Migration may be defined as the movement of people or animals from one geographic place to another in search of better food sources, shelter and/or protection. This movement may be temporary, seasonal or permanent. Jagat Motwani and others have classified Indian emigration trends into three broad categories:[14]

a) ***Classical wave*:** Movements that date back to fifth century

BCE, which include cultural colonization by Hinduism and Buddhism, and early explorations by Indian traders.

b) ***Colonial wave*:** The movement of indentured labourers (to be discussed later in detail).

c) ***Contemporary wave*:** A recent migratory trend that started in the 1960s and is characterized by the "brain drain".

Prakash Jain has categorized the Indian emigration trends into five historical trends:[15]

a) ***Indentured labour emigration*:** This began in the year 1834 and lasted till 1920. In this type of emigration, the emigrant had to sign a contract with the employer to work for three to four years for a specified wage. After the end of the contract, the labourer had the freedom to join any other employer within the colony.

b) ***Kangani* system:** This started in the early nineteenth century and lasted till 1938. The word "*Kangani*" was derived from the Tamil word *kankani* meaning overseer and foreman. Under this system, labourers were free and were not bound by any contract; they were recruited by a *Kangani* who was an Indian immigrant. The workers received advances from the *Kangani* for their preliminary expenses. Most of these labourers went to Burma, Ceylon and Malaysia. The majority were Tamil-speaking Hindus, followed by Muslims, Christians and Sikhs.

c) ***Free or passage emigration*:** This occurred with the emergence of various new opportunities that were developing in colonial India. The emerging market in East Africa, established by the British and other European powers, was the cause of this movement of peoples. Gujaratis and Punjabis were the first to venture forth. The Gujaratis, who established themselves there as "*Dukanwallas*" (shop keepers), were commercially most successful, and eventually monopolized the trade and commerce of this region. Construction of railways and roads in South-east Asia caused another wave of migration from South India. This trend of emigration was characterized by the fact that the emigrants paid for their own passage and were not bound by any contract.

d) ***"Brain drain" or voluntary emigration*:** This movement witnessed a large number of highly skilled, skilled and semi-skilled professionals and workers from India voluntarily immigrating to advanced industrialized countries in Europe, North America and Oceania—mostly to the US, Britain and Canada—for better prospects. The immigrants were mostly educated professionals such as scientists, engineers, nurses, doctors and teachers. The vacuum created by this migration was termed "brain drain". People from various Indian states participated in this movement, however, the Sikh community was the most prominent amongst them.

e) ***Labour migration*:** This emigration pattern was localized to West Asia. The feature of this migration pattern is different to others. The character of this migration patterns is temporary in nature as the majority of countries do not provide naturalization and citizenship rights to the emigrants other than exceptional cases. All migrants will have to sign a contract for their job as well as business. Prakash Jain points out "the first three forms of migration were the colonial phenomena and the last two are the results of the inherent contradiction of post colonial socioeconomic development in India."

The Indian emigration to West Asia is least researched. Myron Weiner described this temporary settlement of Indians in the Gulf region as "incipient diaspora".[16] According to Prakash Jain, the incipient diaspora can be described as "a relatively sizeable group of foreign workers in industrial and oil producing economies who are ethnically distinct from the host population. They are allowed to remain in the host country for a temporary period but they are not entitled to enjoy any rights of a citizen… these foreign workers cannot be categorized as immigrants in the real sense, but the majority of them continue to stay in the host country for indefinite periods of time."[17] The tenure of their stay depends upon the renewal of their respective contracts. The majority of the Indian migrants to the UAE are from the state of Kerala. The reasons for this are many: Gulf countries are closer to Kerala; the earning potential in Gulf countries is higher than that in any of the Indian states; there is an increasing gap between birth and death rates leading to a population increase; many states in India still favour their local regional employees, which hinder opportunities for people from other states; housing, traffic and pollution problems too have caused Keralites to migrate; and lastly, Gulf remittances have made possible better standards of living for those working in the Gulf and their families.[18]

Recently a new interest has emerged in the field of diaspora-led development. The proper utilization of benefit from the "three 'R's"—recruitment, remittance and return—which are all integral aspects of migration that proactively support the economic development of the migrants' home countries, that help tackle diseases and hunger issues, and improve education and financial stability back home. There are, however, certain negatives associated with migration, such as:

a) The elderly family members suffer neglect as the youth and middle-aged leave the homeland
b) Male migration has resulted in an increased burden of running the household singlehandedly on women.
c) Scarcity of skilled and unskilled labour in the homeland.
d) The psychological impact on the emigrants of being away from their families.

It can be argued that economic benefit from migration is higher than the associated cost. This is supported by the fact that despite the costs, the number of emigrants per year keeps increasing. This is applicable to all states across India. The data presented in Table 4.1 supports this argument.

As the data shows in Table 4.1, the number of workers granted emigration from the state of Kerala in the year 2004 was 63,512, which had increased to 1,80,703 by 2008. The same trend is noticed in the case of Uttar Pradesh where the number of emigrants was 27,428 in the year 2004, and in the year 2008 that had increased to 1,39,254. Though in varying degrees, such increase in migration is true for almost all the states listed above. Looking at the above data, emigration seems to be a popular choice. Hence, it would be very useful if the labour-receiving and labour-exporting nations too could co-operate to encourage such migration.

Formation of Indian Diaspora in the Gulf

The Indian subcontinent's linkage with the Gulf and Arab regions, it can be assumed, dates back to the third millennium BCE. This hypothesis of exchange between the two regions has been supported by archaeological findings. Archaeologists have substantiated their argument by establishing the "embellished pottery and seashells recovered from Harappa valley on north India as those belonging to the Dilman civilization of Baharain or the Magan civilization of Oman."[20]

Table 4.1: State-specific figures of workers granted emigration clearance/ ECNR endorsement during the years 2004–08[19]

Sl. No.	*Migration from the State of*	*In 2004*	*In 2005*	*In 2006*	*In 2007*	*In 2008*	*In 2009 (till March 31)*
1.	Kerala	63,512	1,25,075	1,20,083	1,50,475	1,80,703	35,123
2.	Tamil Nadu	1,08,964	1,17,050	1,55,631	1,50,842	1,28,791	22,748
3.	Karnataka	19,237	75,384	24,362	27,014	22,413	5,490
4.	Gujarat	22,218	49,923	13,274	20,066	15,716	2,886
5.	Andhra Pradesh	72,580	48,498	97,680	1,05,044	97,530	18,969
6.	Maharashtra	28,670	29,289	15,356	21,496	24,786	5,458
7.	Punjab	25,302	24,088	39,311	53,942	54,469	7,475
8.	Uttar Pradesh	27,428	22,558	66,131	91,613	1,39,254	34,944
9.	Rajasthan	35,108	21,899	50,236	70,896	64,601	11,320
10.	Bihar	21,812	9,366	36,493	51,805	60,642	13,074
11.	Delhi	6,052	6,024	9,098	5,327	4,512	707
12.	Madhya Pradesh	8,888	5,312	7,047	3,616	2,321	533
13.	West Bengal	8,986	5,102	14,929	24,817	26,094	5,548
14.	Haryana	1,267	2,313	193	1,852	1,779	338
15.	Goa	7,053	1,627	4,063	3,102	2,210	442
16.	Orissa	6,999	1,258	4,114	6,696	8,919	1,795
17.	Others	0	24	1,909	924	0	0
	Total	**464076**	**544790**	**659910**	**789527**	**834740**	**166850**

Source: http://moia.gov.in/writereaddata/pdf/Annual_Report_2008-09.pdf, accessed on April 20, 2010

The strategic location of the Gulf region was favoured by the traders as a point of transshipment. The farsighted Indian and Arab traders of that era realized this advantage of location to deliver goods to and import from the neighbouring states. Besides the archaeological evidence, similarities found in the methods of various activities such as fishing, boat construction, measuring/weighing practiced by the civilizations of these two regions too hint at a long standing platform of trade and commercial and cultural exchange that existed between them.

From what we can deduce from the many Arabic poems from the pre-Islamic era that praised Indic goods and ideas, the Indian subcontinent was well known to the Gulf and Arabic regions historically. For example, back then, a common name for a girl child was "Hind" which was derived from the word "Hindi". It will be safe to assume that Indian presence in this region, though in small numbers, was prevalent. The majority of Indians came to this region either to do business or for employment opportunities to better their economic condition.[21] Nora Muhammad Al-Qasimi also stated that many people from the Indian subcontinent settled in this region before the colonial era. The locals called them *Al Zat*, *Al Asawira*, *Al Syabiha*, *Al Ahamira*, *Al Meed*, *Al Bayasira*, and *Al Takatira*; they shared their trade practices and professionalism with the people of this region. A small community of *Al Zat* still exist in the Boureemi area, who work as goldsmiths, blacksmiths and carpenters. Their service to this region is comparable to the service of the *Banias*. The *Zat* community speaks "Rateeni", however, they are conversant in other languages too.[22]

Indo-Arab commercial transaction flourished during the seventh century CE. The political unification of Arabia with its neighbouring states—Egypt, Iraq, etc.—increased the economic consumption and therefore the demand for Indian commodities. Socio-cultural relations between the Indic and Gulf/Arab regions increased when Sindh and Gujarat became a part of the Arab Islamic Empire. The old political linkage of these two regions with the Arab world helped in the development of the close ties that exist between India and the UAE.

The commercial activities between the Indic and Arab world decreased with the advent of Portugal's domination of the Indian Ocean trade. Arab merchants suffered a setback with the introduction of trade licence and taxes by the Portuguese colonizers. However, Indo-Gulf trade relations renewed when the Indic and Gulf regions became colonies of the British. Until 1947, decisions regarding economic and political affairs in the Gulf were taken and implemented by British authorities in India.[23]

Early History of Indian Migration in the Gulf

From the previous discussion it can be seen that Indo-Gulf trade relations existed long before the discovery of oil in the Gulf and Arab regions. Modern historical evidence suggests that a number of the Indic settlements in this region started from the sixteenth century CE.[24] The commercial activities of the Indians thenceforth increased in this region, especially in Muscat and Oman. According to Allen, "The Portuguese relied heavily on Indian Hindus in their attempt to secure a monopoly of the Indian Ocean and Arabian Gulf trade. The most important trading partner was Thatta of Sindh."[25]

As pointed out earlier, no systematic study has yet been conducted of the Indian presence in the UAE though a few studies conducted recently give a very sketchy picture of the Indian presence in other Gulf states.[26] From the fifteenth century, traders from India started migrating towards West Asian countries.[27] Based on available documents, it can be stated that Indian migration to the Gulf region was a free migration mainly by traders. Indian diasporic communities were largely composed of Gujartis, Sindhis and Lohanas, although Kerala had a more ancient link with this region. Until the discovery of oil, very limited numbers of Indians were present in this area. Gujaratis and Sindhis played a key role in strengthening the commercial ties between these two regions. Most of the Sindhi and Gujarati interviewees claimed that in 711 CE, during the Muslim conquest of India, Sindh and parts of Gujarat had been incorporated into the Arab-Islamic empire. This political linkage provided the platform for Gujaratis and Sindhis to start commercial transactions between these two regions. These "conspicuous Gujaratis" and "ubiquitous Sindhis" possessed a tremendous entrepreneurial drive through which they were able to find their fortunes despite being far away from their homeland. Sometimes they had to venture into areas where no Indians had ever ventured before.[28]

Indian Diaspora in the UAE before the Oil Era

Before the discovery of oil there was a small and thriving Indic community, mostly Sindhis and Gujaratis, who used to bring textiles and gold from their homeland to this region. Today India is the third largest trading partner of the UAE.[29] The strong friendship between these two countries is based on age-old economic and commercial links, and the long history of trading contacts. Due to the paucity of documented resources it is difficult to conclude when these communities had begun to establish diasporic outposts in this region. Although no concrete statistical data can be found to quantify ancient Indian populations in this region, it is an established fact that Indian merchant communities were present in this area from long back.

From ancient times Arabs have had a close connection with the Malabar coast, from where they bought spices, timber and coconut fibre. Timber was used to make the planks for the sides of dhows and sambuqs, and coconut fibre was used to tie the planks of the ship's hull together instead of nails to better survive in the seawater.[30] Early Indic peoples came here as "sojourners". During the eighteenth and nineteenth centuries India and the Gulf reinstated communications considerably as the Perpetual Treaty, signed in 1853 under the British colonial rule, secured these regions. The first Maritime Truce of 1835 was signed between rulers of Dubai, Sharjah, Ajman and Abu Dhabi in an attempt to quell all conflicts at sea, especially during the pearling season. Initially the treaty had a one-year term. In June 1843, a new ten years' treaty was signed which brought stability into this region. The states who signed Perpetual Maritime Truce came to be known as the Trucial States.[31] This incident facilitated Indians to be present in this region either on their own account or as representatives of British and Indian firms.[32]

Classical Indian communities can be classified into two main groups. Khojas and Banias. All Hindu traders were collectively called Banias by the Gulf population. The Hindu immigrants were from Sind and Gujarat, and were mostly engaged in the pearl trade. The number of immigrants was very small; only around 200 Hindus were present in the UAE and they mostly stayed in and around Dubai and Abu Dhabi. These Hindu merchants from India did not bring their families with them. They only stayed for a small period; their migration pattern was circulatory. As a result they could not assimilate properly with the host society. The other activities they were engaged in were the textile business, banking, and money lending.[33]

British presence in the Gulf as a colonial power transformed the activities of the pearling industry. Initially indigenous merchants fixed the price of pearls and invested in the pearling industry. UAE joined the global market when the demand for the "Gulf Pink Pearl" increased in Europe and America. Britain started to control the economy. The Bania merchants who were associated with the British East India Company in India came to this region and started working here as British agents. The presence of Hindu merchants in the Trucial States in the mid-nineteenth century brought about many changes in the social and economic structure of the area. They used to import other basic necessities of life such as cloth, rice, sugar and coffee. The Hindu merchants in Abu Dhabi came from Thatta in Sindh. Their traditional nature kept them alienated from the host society, as their religion, customs and costume were different. On top of this they were associated with Britain as they acted as British representatives in this region.[34] They were the main financiers of the pearl industry in partnership with British entrepreneurs. They used to provide loans to Muslims since Muslims according to Islamic religion are forbidden to practice usury. According to a study presented to the Political Resident by Haji Abdul Latif, the Residency Agent in 1901, "the number of Banias in Dubai was fifty two, in Abu Dhabi thirty nine, in Sharjah seventy six, in Ras Al Khaimah nine, in Ajman four and in Umm Al Qaiwain three".[35]

The other Indian community that also played an important role in the UAE was the Khojas. They used to enjoy British protection. Originally the Khojas were Hindus from Sindh and Kutch, who during the fifteenth century were converted to the Shiah sect of Islam by the Ismailis. They were present mostly in the port areas of the Trucial States. The number of Khojas on the Trucial coast was around 220.[36]

In the year 1930 many Banias went back to India. Two factors were responsible for this: a) the introduction of cultured pearl in the market; b) the great world depression. With the development of the oil industry, immigrants were required as workers for various developmental activities. With the oil boom, the economic condition of this area changed drastically. With increased purchasing power, the local people started demanding various goods. Indian entrepreneurs seized this opportunity and started retail businesses in this region.

It can be argued that the Indian diasporic community contributed a lot to this region. S.B. Miles pointed out that "due to their superior capacity and knowledge of the market they acquired immense fortunes for themselves. They not only served their own purpose, in turn they provided service to all Arab classes as banker, broker, and moneylender."[37] According to Fatma Al-Saygh, "It is therefore the Banias who financed the yearly pearling expedition. In addition the Indian merchants supplied the diving fleets with textiles and imported goods, taking pearls in payment for supplies. They also monopolized shopkeeping and retail trading activities; many became extremely rich. As a result Indians comprised the second biggest economic class in Dubai."[38]

Based on the information stated above, it can be concluded that two main communities of Indian settlers has been present in this region since before the oil era, namely the Banias and Khojas. According to Lorimer, "[o]ut of 70 shops 19 shops were owned by Hindus, later on seven Khoja traders came and stayed in Abu Dhabi."[39] During the mid-nineteenth century they brought their families and settled here permanently. It can be speculated that this small number of Indians exercised enormous influence in the economic sphere. Following

Christine Dobbin, it can be stated that this "microscopic" Indian community acquired extreme control over finance.[40] Though they were socially marginalized, they were highly successful in commercial activities. As mentioned earlier, these Indians could not assimilate culturally with the host society and remained guests to this region throughout their stay. This small community became a role model to Arab entrepreneurs in importing various necessary items to this region. It can be argued that Indians were highly successful due to their hard work, values, commitment, morality, and ethics and were thus catalysts for commerce. During the emergence of the global capital economy in 1980, they played an active role in generating more investment and trade with various countries. Thus we can say that these initial settlers laid the foundation for bilateral relations between UAE and India.

At present, the majority of Indian population in UAE is from Kerala. The rest are from Maharashtra, Goa, Punjab, Uttar Pradesh, Bihar, Rajasthan, and Bengal. The business sector is dominated by Gujaratis and Sindhis.

Table 4.2: Population of Indians living in GCC countries and their relative percentage[41]

Country	*Total Population (in millions)*	*Total Indian population*	*Percentage of Indians to Total Population*	*Total expatriate population*	*Percentage of Indians among expatriates*
Bahrain	1.04	359,000	34.52%	510,000	70.39%
Kuwait	3.44	590,000	17.15%	2,340,000	25.21%
Oman	3.20	600,000	17.44%	1,000,000	60.00%
Qatar	1.62	500,000	30.86%	870,000	53.70%
Saudi Arabia	24.50	1,800,000	7.35%	7,000,000	25.71%
UAE	6.00	1,750,000	29.17%	3,600,000	48.61%
	39.80	5,599,000	22.74%	15,320,000	36.55%

Source: Bahrain–www.e.gov.bh; Qatar–Government Statistics Authority; Kuwait, Oman and Saudi Arabia–Concerned Indian Embassies; U.A.E–www.uaedirect.com

The early Indian settlers present in this region since before the discovery of oil played a key role in this increase, as recorded above in Table 4.2, bringing the Indian population in UAE to 1,750,000.[42] They dominated the business scene in this region for centuries. During the period 1830–1950, migrations from India to this region were "temporary" in nature. As most of them were "sojourners" and their presence in various parts of the world was circulatory, the question might arise as to whether or not to include this migratory group within the category of diaspora. This group, however, helps us trace back to the Indian presence in the UAE since before the discovery of oil; they did not form a diaspora, but their presence in and contribution to this region did pave the way for the present generation of Indian diasporic peoples settled in the UAE. The history of the migration process represents the fact that "Migration begets Migration; one Migration will be followed by another Migration."[43] As Roger Ballard rightly pointed out, "Migration invariably precipitates a transnational networks, which operate in a least two distinct but mutually complimentary ways.... [T]he process of chain migration to which such networks give rise a kind of long distance escalator which enables those who are in a position to step on to them can thereby be transported out of the positions of relative poverty in which they would otherwise have been confined, and to take advantage of the radically enhanced patterns of opportunity available elsewhere. When the lower end of the escalator is located amongst very small-scale peasant farmers in the third world, whilst the upper end reaches into metropolitan cities in the developed world, the advantage which accrues from stepping aboard are immense...."[44]

In order to understand the dynamism of the initial Indian settlers, let us take a glimpse into their milieu back then, in which they had to start up and operate their businesses. A sketch of the early conditions can be retrieved from the personal accounts of prominent Indian businessmen in this region, such as Mohan Jashanmal, Ram Buxani, Magangal Pancholia and K.M. Bhatia. Magangal Pancholia, the owner of the Arabian Trading Agency and one of the most prominent businessmen in Dubai, recounts: "Life in Dubai and UAE in those days was not like it is today. It was very difficult to live. There were no toilets near the marketplace in Dubai. People primarily travelled by sea to reach Abu Dhabi from Dubai and sometimes even rode on camels and donkeys, the other transport medium commonly used to commute between Dubai and Sharjah." As P.V. Vivekanand describes in his book: "Since there were no air conditioners, residents would prefer to sleep on the terrace. Dew drops falling fresh in the morning would wake them up and they would go inside the house for a couple more winks before waking up again to start their daily chores. Indians used to live in small rooms, and they made bread and washed clothes all in one single room. Every item of daily use was imported from India and Iran. Vegetables were rarely available. Rich people moved around on donkeys which were rare enough to be considered a status symbol."[45]

In those days buildings were made of local lime and stones. The rent of an average ten by fifteen feet house was around Rs 10 per month. "Still 'Souk Al Banin' or the Merchant Bazaar in Dubai was the nerve centre of our existence," states Vasanti Sundaram.[46] All these entrepreneurs should be credited for their farsightedness. In spite of various challenges in the UAE in those days their farsightedness prompted them to land and, eventually, settle in this region. Due to their skill in business they could visualize this area as a global trading centre. This powerful business group established themselves as a successful community in Lingah on the Strait of Hormuz. Lingah was an established trading centre of the pearl business. The Indian businessmen were active in this region till 1874, when Lingah was still under the control of the Arab Tribal administration. With Iran taking control of this area and imposing high customs duties on trading, the Indian communities of Lingah searched for an alternative place for trade and shifted their businesses from Lingah to Dubai. In 1984, the then ruler of Dubai, His Highness Sheikh Maktoum Bin Hasher al Makthoum, invited the Indians of Lingah to come and settle in the Emirates.[47] The Sindhi community claims that Thatta, then a part of British India, had a long commercial link with the Arab region. Arab traders used to visit Thatta frequently, sold pearls there and bought handmade cloth and spices, Eventually, the Arabs invited these Sindhis to be partners with them in business, a link that facilitated them to visit and explore this unknown region. Later on they started settling permanently in this region, making it their second home. The lack of reliable statistical data hinders the process of quantifying the role played by this semi-permanent diaspora. However, this does not impair the fact that these pre-oil era Indian Sojourners did indeed lay the foundation for the formation of the modern Indian diaspora in the UAE, that their networking skills played a key role in their own successes as well as towards the formation of this diaspora.[48] Most of the Indian migrants in the UAE today support this argument.

Their position and prestige in the UAE did not come easy to the Indian community. Most of the interviewees stated that it was their values that earned them the position they held today. Trust also played a key role in business transactions as there was no system of issuing receipts for transactions; both parties kept a record of the consignments on the basis of which payments were settled every Saturday. This practice was called "*Sambedi*", *Sambe* being the Iranian word for Saturday. There have never been any disputes from any of the parties in business regarding any discrepancy in settlement of payments.

According to Pancholia, when their ancestors first landed in this region almost three hundred years ago, they did not even enjoy the basic amenities of life.[49] In 1953, Grey McKenzie installed the first generator at Sheikh Saeed's palace, and electricity reached the business area only in 1960.[50] Wells were the main source of water. Each well provided water only for one week. Diggers received one Rupee per well. River water was brought in from Basra (Iraq) via the sea in launches, in four-gallon kerosene containers. Water fetched from wells was salty and hence needed to be strained and kept in Persian pots before it could be consumed.[51] Movies were the main source of entertainment. There was only one open air theatre at Al Nasr Square that screened only one movie per night. Every moviegoer used to carry a blanket with them to protect themselves from cold while watching the movie in the open air at night.[52]

In spite of all these hardships faced by the old Indian communities in the UAE, it was their virtues—honesty, sincerity, perseverance, compassion, and simple living—that made them succeed. Most of the interviewees acknowledged the fact that despite all hindrances the many positive aspects of the UAE economy is what kept them going. The strategic location of Dubai as a re-exporting centre of goods and services to neighbouring states gave the Indian business communities the opportunity to market goods and services brought from India. Starting from the reign of the East India Company, the rupee was in currency and was accepted here till the 1960s.[53]

Entrepreneurs in those days enjoyed total freedom in doing business in the UAE. With the formation of the Dubai Municipality in 1961 the system of registration of shops under given names and issuing business licenses started. The procedure of getting a license was simple. The businessman was only required to show either a shop or warehouse or just express his intention of doing business. The license fee was Rs 100.[54] The concept of local partnership was introduced in 1970 when UAE became a Federation, whereby to form a limited liability company it became mandatory that foreign equity share should not exceed forty-nine per cent while fifty-one per cent of the shares had to be held by a UAE national. These local partners or agents were not to be directly involved in the business operations but were to be involved in other activities such as issuing visas, labour cards, etc. In return they received a percentage of the profit or turnover. However, in various cases this stringency was waived by the ruler. As was pointed out by Pancholia, "I took the initiative to approach His Highness Sheikh Hamdam bin Rashid Al Maktoum, Deputy Ruler of Dubai and the UAE Minister of Finance and Industry, seeking his help over the issue. He magnanimously waived the clause for one hundred and fifty long time traders in our community.... In 1920, there were about 20,000 residents in the small Indian communities where everyone knew each other."[55]

This favourable disposition towards Indians was the result of the cumulative contribution made by the Indian community in the UAE since early times. This is better understood by a comment made by Mirza Hussain Al Sayegh, Secretary to His Highness Sheikh Hamdan Bin Rashid Al Maktoum, "The nationals are aware that Indian community has a valuable contribution to commerce and industry and are working very close."[56] He also commented that these Indians paid their duties, rents, the license and custom fees regularly and the Government has had no complaints whatsoever against these Indians. The Indian merchant class not only provided various goods and services to the local people but also significantly helped develop the infrastructure of this region. In those days the income of the UAE government was not very high. According to Pancholia, "They also provided ration of rice, coffee, tea, sugar, ghee and spices to the pearl drivers to sustain them during their three-month seasonal trip. The families that were left behind were also taken care of with a supply of similar provisions."[57] Indian merchants used to purchase pearls from local Arab merchants (*tawash*). At that time customs duty was four point six percent. Customs duty was imposed on imported cloth according to the number of cartons being imported.[58] In those days the four main alien communities in Dubai were Indians, Pakistanis, Iranians and Baluchis. Over time the Indians in particular managed to transcend by transforming their commercial relationships into personal relationships and acquired a special position within UAE society. Due to a bettering relationship between certain Indian entrepreneurs and the local Arabs, some prominent businessmen were even allowed to own properties in this region. Besides, the two major factors that helped the Indian entrepreneurs strengthen their position in this region during the period 1900–2000 were growth in the pearl trade, and the emergence of Dubai in 1903 as an important port to this region.[59]

In spite of their hardships the Indian diasporic peoples of the UAE have proved themselves to be a valuable asset to both their home and host countries. Any analysis will be incomplete without an understanding of their dynamism of the early emigrant to the UAE. In order to understand this Indian presence in the region and to acquire a clear view of how they came here, an understanding of how they were placed in the historical record as well as the process of social, economic and political development of this region will be presented next in this chapter.

Pre-Oil Era

Massive oil and gas reserves were discovered in this region in 1958, transforming the economy. However, international oil companies had started oil exploration in this region since 1934 and 1936. The first concession was awarded to Petroleum Development (Trucial Coast) Limited in 1937.[60] An increased presence of European population in this region created a demand for foreign goods. Indian merchants seized this opportunity to cater to their needs and further established themselves as a useful business group. The demand for administrative personnel required for the newly established oil industries also brought various technicians and clerks from India to this region.

But going back to the pre-oil era, it can be conclusively stated that the geographical proximity shared by India and Arabia had caused cultural and commercial exchange between them that dates back to over four thousand years. Further, according to James Olney, since the Gulf was the extension of the British Empire, "Arabia fell within the economic and cultural orbit of India during British Raj whilst it also fell within the political orbit of India. Between 1820–1947, political affairs were dominated by the East India Company and its successor, the British Government of India."[61] Since Arabia was the westernmost frontier of the British Indian Empire, it also served as a buffer zone protecting the Raj and its communication line from the advances of their enemies. The British controlled the Arabian frontier through a policy of maintaining Protectorates.[62]

The political officials were diplomats employed by the British who resided near the foreign State, and imperial officials who were called British Residents and Agents. These "Residents" or "Native Agents"—otherwise known as Honorary Consuls or compradors—were mostly men from wealthy Indian, Arab and Persian merchant families. Arab rulers used to collaborate with these Residents to acquire protection.

Britain used to informally control this empire through this British Native Agency system—a collaborative power triangle which comprised Residents, Native Agents and the local rulers.[63]

The lack of a governing body enforcing order and ensuring universal security provided the Gulf Residents with the chance to exercise an informal control over this region. And since they represented the East Indian Company they enjoyed protection and empowerment provided by the British Raj. Most of them were IPS personnel who came from India, though the numbers of Indians were small. Till the nineteenth century most of the Native Agents in the Gulf were Indians; later on Arabs and Persians were employed as Native Agents.[64]

The relationship between Sheikhdoms and these Native Agents was based on cultural sanction. On the basis of Arabian custom of *dakhala*, the Resident played the role of the *Nujawwir*—which means the protector in Arabic. As the relationship was based on eastern Arabian culture, it can be stated that the relationship was not solely treaty-based. From the ruler's standpoint this Resident was so influential and powerful that he was given the most respected title *Rais-Al-Khaliz* (Chief of the Gulf) and *Fakhamat-Al-Rais* (also meaning Chief). "Because the Pax Britanica was beneficial to the security and economy of the Gulf Sheikhdoms, it was to a large extent self-enforcing."[65] This setup prevailed until 1971 when Britain withdrew its military power from the Gulf.

Merchants who were Native Agents used to enjoy a high status and influence compared to others. These merchants-cum-Native Agents used to enjoy privileges equal to those of the British merchants. According to Lord Curzon if the Resident was the "uncrowned king of the Persian Gulf, then the Native Agents were the Gulf's uncrowned princes."[66]

The benefits enjoyed by the Native Agents were immense; however, they had to encounter many problems too. They faced the threat of being removed from the post by an unsupportive Resident. They also ran the risk of being attacked by those who did not like the British presence in this region. In spite of the problems associated with the Native Agency System, most of the native agents preferred to be under the British protection to enhance their business strength. "The British recruited their first Native Agents from the local Bania community in both the India and the Gulf.[67] The local rulers of the UAE had a close financial relationship with local Bania community.

The Indian merchants had thorough knowledge of the political and socio-cultural systems and languages in this area. For these reasons they were favoured and recruited by the British as Native Agents. Another reason behind the deployment of these Indians as Native Agents was the harsh geographic and climatic conditions of this region that were not favoured by the European members of the British administration. Other than this, the non-Europeans were willing to work for a lower salary than that drawn by their European counterparts working in the same positions.[68] The Bania community seized this opportunity and established their businesses in the UAE.

From an economic point of the view, the Gulf Sheikhdom did not hold much importance to British India, except for the pearl trade. During the seventeenth and eighteenth century, trade and shipping between the Sheikhdom and British India was controlled by the local Arabs, Persians and the Indian merchants. On this basis it can be stated that the Indian merchants played a key role in developing trade between UAE and India. According to Frauke Heard-Bay, a prominent UAE historian, the total value of imports across the Trucial Coast was worth 2.5 million rupees on average.[69] This was at the turn of the century. The most prominent items were grains, pulses and clothes from India.[70]

In 1962 the British Indian Steam Navigation Company started shipping between Basaiah and Bombay. Muscat which is in a neighbouring state of the UAE had a link with British India since 1862 when various ports were incorporated into the BI line. Dubai was incorporated into this network in the year 1904 and Sharjah in 1932.[71] After 1860, the government of India encouraged trade between these two regions. In the year 1970, Indo-UAE trade value was $180 million per annum and it has increased up to $29,023.68 million in the year 2007–08. After the discovery of oil in this region the trade link got strengthened for mutual benefit. Imperial Airways (presently known as British Airways) later on established an airfield in the UAE. Britain maintained its presence in this region till even after India's Independence.[72]

Post-Oil Era

The exploration of massive oil reserves enabled the UAE to embark on various developmental projects. However, to start with, this budding oil industry faced an acute shortage of labourers as their national workforce was inadequate compared to the large-scale requirements. The majority of this workforce was used to traditional activities and very few of them were skilled enough to partake in such modern developmental projects. With the increase in demand for semiskilled and skilled workers, the size of the Indian diaspora also increased.

The increase in oil prices furthered their oil revenue. This resulted in economic diversification in the UAE whereby this excess oil revenue was channelled towards various other developmental projects. These other developmental activities also brought about a change in the nature of migration.

Number of Indians in the UAE

Collecting exact data on Indian émigrés in the UAE is not an easy task. UAE became independent in 1971. Hence, documentation of official data by the UAE government has only started recently. Based on available data it can be assumed that there has been a steep increase in the population Indian émigrés in the UAE during the period of discovery of oil in this region. Table 4.3 below is the current data which shows that numbers of Indians are higher compared to other nationalities.

To further my argument it must be stated that the capabilities of Indians are also acknowledged by GCC countries .The percentage of Indians is the highest, followed by Pakistanis and Egyptians. According to the opinion of UAE Ambassador Talmiz Ahmad, the Indian diaspora in the UAE can be represented as follows:

a) **1970–80**: The infrastructural development phase. India started dominating the labour market. So the number of blue-collar workers increased to between 75 per cent and 80 per cent and the professionals by 5 per cent.
b) **1990**: Development of non-oil sector and service sector. This period needed professionals for maintenance work. So the number of Indian professionals increased to between 25 per cent and 30 per cent.

Talmiz Ahmed, the Indian ambassador to the UAE for 2007–2010, expects the knowledge-based economy to flourish by the year 2012. It is expected that the number of Indian professionals in the UAE will increase and the number of diasporic labourers will decrease to 35–40 per cent. White collar non-professionals will be replaced by UAE nationals. So the Emiritization policy is not going to affect

Table 4.3: Indians in comparison with other nationality émigrés in the Arab countries [73]

Country	*Indians*	*Pakistanis*	*Egyptians*	*Philippinnes*	*Bangladeshis*	*Sinhalese*	*Others*	*Total*
Bahrain	359,000	60,000	20,000	50,000	50,000	20,000	40,000	510,000
Kuwait	590,000	130,000	420,000	125,000	215,000	100,000	760,000	2,340,000
Oman	600,000	100,000	20,000	40,000	160,000	20,000	60,000	1,000,000
Qatar	500,000	90,000	60,000	120,000	70,000	30,000	0	870,000
Saudi Arabia	1,800,000	1,250,000	800,000	800,000	1,200,000	300,000	150,000	7,000,000
UAE	1,750,000	1,200,000	250,000	800,000	500,000	230,000	200,000	3,600,000
Total	**5,599,000**	**2,830,000**	**1,570,000**	**1,935,000**	**2,195,000**	**700,000**	**1,210,000**	**15,320,000**

Source: Qatar-Government statistics authority, Kuwait, Oman, Saudi Arabia, Concerned Indian embassies—www.uaedirect.com (UAE); www.e.gov.bh (Bahrain)

Table 4.4: Percentage of the total GCC population [74]

Indians	*Pakistanis*	*Egyptians*	*Philippinnes*	*Bangladeshis*	*Sinhalese*	*Others*	*Total*
35%	18%	10%	12%	14%	4%	7%	100%

Source: www.uaedirect.com

Indian professionals as foreign professionals and maintenance workers will be required in this region. Moreover, India has been meeting the human resource needs of the UAE and other Arab nations of this region for decades and centuries, which have resulted in the present, mutually respected close ties.

In the UAE, with 65 per cent of them belonging to the blue collar category, only 12 per cent belonging to white collar category, and 23 per cent comprising of professional and family members, there are more blue collar Indian employees compared to professionals and white collar employees. It is expected that the demand for workers in the non-oil sector and service sector will increase in the UAE and the number of professionals is expected to increase up to 25–30 percent.[75]

Table 4.5: Profile of the Indian Population in the GCC Countries (source same as Table 4.3)

Country	*Blue Collar Employees (%)*	*White Collar Employees (%)*	*Professional Family Members (%)*
Bahrain	230,000 (70)	66,000 (20)	33,000 (10)
Kuwait	460,000 (78)	30,000 (5)	100,000 (17)
Oman	400,000 (66)	100,000 (17)	100,000 (17)
Qatar	350,000 (70)	75,000 (15)	75,000 (15)
KSA	1,242,000 (69)	180,000 (10)	378,000(21)
UAE	1,138,000 (65)	216,000 (12)	414,000 (23)
Total	**3,820,000 (68)**	**667,000 (12)**	**1,100,000 (20)**

Source: Qatar-Government statistics authority, Kuwait, Oman, Saudi Arabia, Concerned Indian embassies—www.uaedirect.com (UAE); www.e.gov.bh (Bahrain)

Prospects of the Indian Diaspora in the UAE

The presence of Indian diasporic peoples can be felt in every field of the UAE economy. They have played a key role in the diverse developmental processes of the UAE .There is a large number of well established diasporic Indian entrepreneurs whose contribution towards this region has been paramount. The Indian communities here are respected for their professionalism and reliability. For centuries the Sindhi and Gujarati communities dominated this region's trade with Arab partners.[76]

Recently the Government of UAE has undertaken various measures to replace expatriates with nationals.

a) The UAE government has adopted a policy of gradual Emiratization which will be replacing foreigners with UAE nationals who are qualified to meet the requirements. The growing number of educated nationals are trying to get various managerial positions in the oil and banking sectors.
b) Demographic imbalances and cultural pollution have been given as another cause of reduction of foreigners from this region.

Thus the Indian migrant labourers are at the receiving end at present. Yet the "Gulf-El Dorado syndrome" is still prevalent among Indians. However, it is expected that the demand for professionals and technically qualified Indians will continue to rise. Indian professionals are most sought after in knowledge-based sectors such as Dubai Internet City, Dubai Media City, etc.

Table 4.6: Percentage of Indians from various states in India living in GCC Countries (rounded off to the nearest hundred)[77]

Country	*Kerala Population (%)*	*Tamil Nadu Population (%)*	*Andhra Pradesh Population (%)*	*Karnataka Population (%)*	*Others Population (%)*
Bahrain	198,000 (55)	54,000 (15)	36,000 (10)	13,000 (4)	52,800 (16)
Kuwait	260,000 (39)	80,000 (13.5)	110,000 (17)	40,000 (7)	107,000 (18)
Oman	300,000 (50)	100,000 (17)	120,000 (20)	40,000 (6.5)	40,000 (6.5)
Qatar	335,000 (67)	40,000 (8)	60,000 (12)	25,000 (5)	40,000 (8)
KSA	810,000 (45)	450,000 (25)	270,000 (15)	90,000 (5)	180,000 (10)
UAE	962,500 (55)	320,000 (20)	128,000 (8)	128,000 (8)	144,000 (9)
Total	2,760,000* (51)	1,068,500* (20)	586,000* (11)	320,200* (6)	615,000* (12)

Source: www.uaedirect.com; Courtesy: Indian Embassy in the UAE.

The above table shows that the majority of Indians in the UAE came from South Indian states—Kerala accounts for 55 percent, Tamil Nadu accounts for 20 percent, Andhra Pradesh accounts for 8 percent, Karnataka accounts for 8 per cent and other states comprise 9 percent. It can be speculated that the presence of Keralites in the UAE in such numbers is owing to Kerala's age-old contact with West Asia and the Middle East which dates back to 3000 BCE. A brief summary of the ancient connection will help us understand Kerala's dominance in this region. Muziris, in Kerala, was an eminent sea port through which pepper, cinnamon, cardamom, ginger and other spices were exported to the West.[78] This link facilitated the Keralites to come to this region through their personal contacts—friends, relatives, agents. Most of them belong to the category of "small-time" traders. The Muslim population represents a larger number than Christians and Hindus. There are 56 per cent Sunni Muslims, 26 per cent Christians, and 16 per cent Hindus.[79]

The number of Keralites in this region started increasing since the British presence in this area. Most of them worked as clerks. Their proficiency in English language landed them administrative work. Few of them were shopkeepers. Today there are many skilled and unskilled labourers here who are from Kerala. Recently, Yusuf Ali M.A., a renowned entrepreneur in the UAE, originally from Kerala, received the Padmashree Award for having contributed a lot towards the development of bilateral relations between India and UAE. A case study about him will be presented at the end of the study.

The presence of Tamils in the UAE is smaller compared to people from other South Indian states. Some of them are employed in high positions, and a few in clerical jobs, however, a majority of the Tamils here are labourers.

Before the year 1970, the Sikh community was very small in this region. But their presence here increased during the oil boom. They mainly work here as technicians, carpenters, electricians, and masons. Presently, some also have their own businesses here, such as air-conditioning and contracting.

Initially, Indian migration to the Gulf, and especially to the UAE, occurred due to a shortage of indigenous skilled and semi-skilled workforce in these regions. A group of highly skilled and educated professionals and unskilled labourers came to this region for betterment of their lives. Based on what this study learned from the community-wide interviews conducted during 2008 and other sources, it can be stated that about 30 per cent of the total population and over 50 per cent of the workforce in the UAE today are Indians; they are the largest expatriate community in the UAE. The Indian community of the UAE can be presented as follows:

a) Unskilled workers: Employed by construction companies, municipalities, agricultural firms, and also as domestic helps;
b) Skilled and semi-skilled workers;
c) Professionals: Doctors, Engineers, Accountants, employed in government and private sectors;
d) Businessmen.

The nature of Indian migration in the UAE could also be analysed on the basis of the duration of their stay. Most of them stay on a temporary basis. The percentage of long-term settlers is very small. Indians in the UAE fall under a different category compared to the Indians émigrés in other countries. The UAE Citizenship Law does not offer permanent residency to Indians. However as an exception, some Indians, although very few, did receive citizenship rights in the UAE. Generally, the position of Indians in the UAE is as "guest workers". The number of male migrants is higher than female migrants. Most male migrants do not bring their families over due to various factors that make life very unstable in the host country.

According to the government of the UAE, FNC members and nationals, the presence of non-national workforce, whose numbers are higher than the nationals of the UAE, is contributing towards a demographic imbalance in the country. As a result, nationals are getting marginalized in their own country. Hence, to revert the situation, the Ministry of Labour and Social Affairs of the UAE has undertaken an Emiratization policy whereby all public positions held by foreign workers will be replaced with UAE nationals. Private companies are also being advised by the UAE government to employ more nationals in place of expatriate workers.[80] But, in spite of various attempts made by the government, deploying the Emiritization policy remains a major challenge. According to the latest estimated figures released by TANMIA (The National Human Resource Development and Employment Authority), the UAE population is expected to increase to 7.557 million in 2010 compared to the figure of 5.631 million that was speculated in 2006; the total number of UAE nationals then will not be more than 1.5 million.[81]

There is a discrepancy in the private sector between the jobs available and the recruitment. There are more jobs available than the employable national workforce. There is a lack of adequate expertise among the job applicants and an unrealistic expectation of the job benefits on their behalf. This demographic imbalance and cultural pollution have been cited as the reason for the implementation of such a policy. Yet the demand for professionals and technically sound Indian job applicants remains.

Status of Indians in the UAE

***Gender Basis*:** In the UAE, the number of females in the immigrant population is less compared to their male counterparts. One of the reasons is fewer work opportunities for women; the only jobs available for women are nursing, teaching and domestic services. The other reason for less representation of women could be attributed to the culture of Indian society. Very rarely is independent female migration encouraged by Indian families. Also, as stated earlier, low-income group labourers do not bring their families with them as the UAE laws do not allow migrants below a prescribed salary level to do that. Other factors, such as higher rents, lack of educational facilities for children, etc., also discourage Indians to bring their families to the UAE.

***Age and Marital Characteristics*:** The majority of Indians settled in the UAE belong to the age group of thirty to forty years and are single. However, little is known as to why this is the case. According to the Commerce Research Bureau of Kerala (1978) 79 per cent of the Keralite migrants in the UAE are about thirty five years of age.[82]

***Economic and Social Status*:** The socio-economic condition of the middle class and the entrepreneurs is different from that of the working class. The former classes enjoy a community life with various associations formed among themselves in accordance with their needs. Weiner states that Indians, though part of the economic structure in UAE, are not a part of the social structure there. Very little social contact exists between the Arabs and the expatriates. But the working class are not allowed to stay in the residential area; they mostly stay in their labour camps away from the city.

The Indians mostly claim that they find themselves more comfortable in Dubai than in Abu Dhabi. Indian food and entertainment are highly appreciated in Dubai; Dubai is even said to be a miniature version of Mumbai.

***The Cultural and Religious Scenario*:** More than a hundred Indian cultural and literary associations are active in the UAE. In Abu Dhabi itself six associations are registered with the government. There are two registered associations in Dubai and another one registered for the other Emirates. The non-registered associations have to get an affiliation with a registered government body. These associations conduct various cultural activities.

Religious activities though are restricted for the non-Muslim population. There are many churches for the Christian community in various places in the Emirates. In Dubai there is one Hindu temple and a *gurdwara*. In Abu Dhabi the construction of temples or *gurdwaras* is not allowed by the government, although *bhajans* and *kirtans* are frequent events in private houses.

***Educational Opportunities*:** More than thirty Indian schools are operating in the UAE, affiliated with the CBSE Board, or other Indian Boards such as the Kerala Board, etc. Recently, many Indian Institutes and Universities have started operations in the Dubai Academic Village. Institutes such as the Birla Institute of Technology, Mahatma Gandhi Universuty (off campus), Mahe Manipal have attracted many students from India. The safety and security alongside future prospects in this region have motivated many Indian students to pursue their academics here.

***Contribution of Indian Diaspora*:** The Indian community in Dubai, Sharjah and Abu Dhabi has formed various registered associations which provide the Indian diaspora in the UAE the needed platform for various opportunities. The Indian Business Professional Group, Abu Dhabi; the Indian Business Council, Dubai; the Indian Sports Club; and the Indian Overseas Forum, Dubai—they play a key role in facilitating interactions between Indian commercial delegates and local influential businessmen.

The Indian diaspora in the UAE has made a huge contribution to the Indian economy. A substantial amount of foreign exchange is remitted to India by the Indian diaspora. Though the official figures of remittance are difficult to get, it is estimated that $2 billion is received annually from the Indian diaspora in the UAE. Approximately $25–7 billion is sent globally as remittance by the Indian diaspora of this region.[83] For example, remittance made through the Bank of Baroda is represented in Table 4.7.

The Table 4.7 reveals that despite a global economic recession, the remittance amount sent to India by the Indians from the UAE

Table 4.7: Remittance data provided by Bank of Baroda

Remittance (in million)	*2006–07*	*2007–08*	*2008–09*	*2009–10*
INR	₹1277.95	₹2073	₹2638	₹2749
USD	$347	$564	$718	$748

Source: Data provided by Bank of Baroda, Abu Dhabi branch.

through the Bank of Baroda has been increasing; from $347 million in FY 2006–07 to $748 million in FY 2009–10.[84]

The non-resident Indian population in the UAE have always contributed to various fields, as summarized below:[85]

a) IDBI Flexi Bond: ₹ 6 crores
b) Various schemes of UTI: ₹16 crores
c) Bank of Baroda Bond (February 1996): ₹25 crores
d) Bank of Baroda Equity Issue (16th December1996): ₹50 crores
e) Resurgent India Bonds: $1.26 billion (total collection: $4.16 billion)
f) Indian Millennium Deposit Scheme (2000): $2 billion

Remittances

Due to paucity of available records on the total amount of remittances provided by the Indian diaspora in the UAE, the study had to depend on the figures of remittance retrieved from the UAE Exchange Centre, the largest currency dealer in the UAE. According to Mr Sudhir Shetty, General Manager, UAE Exchange Centre, the share of the UAE Exchange Centre comes to about sixty per cent of the total volume of the businesses in the UAE.

Tables 4.8, 4.9 and 4.10 clearly show that despite the economic downturn, remittances sent by Indians from the UAE have been increasing. In the year 2009, it was '193,322,082,896 and by April 2010, the amount of remittance was '56,320,970,622 for the year 2010 depicting an upward trend in remittance being sent in by Indians from the UAE. The state-wise data shows that the maximum contribution was made by Kerala, followed by Tamil Nadu, Punjab, Andhra Pradesh, Uttar Pradesh, etc. One of the highlights of this study is the immense contribution made by this Indian diaspora in the UAE towards the Indian economy.

Table 4.8 : Remittance Volume and Counts from UAE to India from UAE Exchange Centre

Year	Total Txns	Vol in USD	Vol in AED	Vol in INR
2006	3,994,034	2,268,513,560	8,333,384,564	102,468,757,523
2007	4,624,175	2,901,171,003	10,657,451,678	119,267,139,915
2008	6,117,058	4,302,837,709	15,806,474,323	187,947,951,115
2009	6,369,558	4,005,845,066	14,715,471,851	193,322,082,896
2010 (till April)	1,935,627	1,243,837,690	4,569,237,756	56,320,970,622

Source: B.R. Shetty, Chairman, UAE Exchange

Table 4.9: Remittance Volume and Counts from UAE to India, UAE Exchange records for the year 2009

State	Counts	Volume in AED	Volume in USD	Volume in INR
Kerala	2,435,627	5,281,056,752	1,437,609,025	69,392,788,614
Tamil Nadu	1,072,663	2,120,210,023	577,163,474	27,859,440,416
Punjab	601,036	1,162,098,772	316,346,474	15,269,912,485
Andhra Pradesh	546,960	1,197,396,112	325,955,114	15,733,717,552
Uttar Pradesh	356,846	618,606,510	168,397,036	8,128,454,739
Maharashtra	319,710	1,628,505,906	443,311,802	21,398,475,993
Karnataka	280,140	798,995,639	217,502,556	10,498,757,750
Bihar	224,072	349,283,552	95,081,952	4,589,566,223
Rajasthan	112,112	271,792,645	73,987,381	3,571,340,070
West Bengal	86,931	204,095,776	55,558,943	2,681,807,011
Gujarat	84,521	303,416,917	82,596,139	3,986,881,222
Goa	78,357	160,973,718	43,820,258	2,115,185,602
Delhi	53,656	330,147,669	89,872,783	4,338,121,791
Orissa	31,901	59,310,350	16,145,461	779,334,662
Himachal Pradesh	21,144	52,352,561	14,251,412	687,909,702
Haryana	20,558	91,988,677	25,041,153	1,208,726,041
Jharkhand	18,629	39,645,142	10,792,199	520,934,936
Pondicherry	13,567	39,701,801	10,807,622	521,679,425
Madhya Pradesh	13,113	53,990,887	14,697,397	709,437,219
Uttaranchal	8,676	25,010,940	6,808,477	328,642,350
Jammu Kashmir	7,081	27,394,734	7,457,393	359,965,261
Assam	4,645	9,129,624	2,485,266	119,962,751
Anywhere Payout	4,270	6,845,275	1,863,421	89,946,534
Chhattisgarh	4,253	10,578,919	2,879,793	139,006,395
Chandigarh	4,014	15,691,274	4,271,478	206,182,462
Union Territory	2,138	2,893,401	787,641	38,019,127
Tripura	940	2,312,737	629,573	30,389,241
Manipur	569	1,038,317	282,651	13,643,422
Lakshadweep	443	1,652,059	449,723	21,707,956
Andaman Nicobar	441	726,530	197,776	9,546,566
Dadra Nagar Haveli	434	796,534	216,833	10,466,415
Meghalaya	431	812,290	221,121	10,673,440
Sikkim	366	663,741	180,683	8,721,516
Daman Diu	353	867,492	236,149	11,398,794
Arunachal Pradesh	260	314,336	85,569	4,130,357
Nagaland	207	328,417	89,402	4,315,376
Mizoram	88	172,017	46,826	2,260,287
Total:	**6,411,152**	**14,870,798,045**	**4,048,127,956**	**195,401,449,703**

Source: B.R. Shetty, Chairman, UAE Exchange

Table 4.10: Remittance Volume and Counts from UAE to India, UAE Exchange records for the year 2010 (till April).

State	*Counts*	*Volume in AED*	*Volume in USD*	*Volume in INR*
Kerala	726,563	1,596,980,116	434,729,853	19,685,654,575
Tamil Nadu	321,675	640,784,511	174,434,330	7,898,822,549
Punjab	181,691	359,504,227	97,864,224	4,431,536,723
Andhra Pradesh	168,779	367,435,497	100,023,274	4,529,303,905
Uttar Pradesh	120,527	207,944,402	56,606,615	2,563,289,060
Maharashtra	99,687	519,745,762	141,485,167	6,406,802,089
Karnataka	89,128	251,423,921	68,442,608	3,099,252,398
Bihar	66,282	108,357,775	29,497,149	1,335,704,628
Rajasthan	35,731	89,533,803	24,372,888	1,103,665,288
West Bengal	28,124	70,875,079	19,293,611	873,662,926
Gujarat	26,625	109,087,554	29,695,809	1,344,700,468
Goa	17,102	40,207,258	10,945,218	495,626,832
Delhi	16,389	108,374,160	29,501,609	1,335,906,599
Orissa	11,446	20,419,175	5,558,507	251,703,089
Himachal Pradesh	6,739	17,777,632	4,839,426	219,141,315
Haryana	6,538	27,165,970	7,395,119	334,869,483
Jharkhand	5,996	12,514,932	3,406,814	154,269,063
Pondicherry	4,890	12,471,435	3,394,973	153,732,887
Madhya Pradesh	4,394	23,593,370	6,422,586	290,830,754
Uttaranchal	3,039	8,460,554	2,303,132	104,291,562
Jammu Kashmir	2,221	8,839,276	2,406,227	108,959,990
Assam	1,360	2,885,224	785,415	35,565,577
Anywhere Payout	498	831,367	226,315	10,248,090
Chhattisgarh	1,376	3,482,340	947,963	42,926,113
Chandigarh	1,057	6,144,698	1,672,709	75,744,464
Union Territory	0	0	0	0
Tripura	332	633,558	172,467	7,809,738
Manipur	161	368,127	100,211	4,537,822
Lakshadweep	191	850,387	231,492	10,482,544
Andaman Nicobar	119	165,258	44,987	2,037,105
Dadra Nagar Haveli	117	228,049	62,080	2,811,120
Meghalaya	142	234,033	63,709	2,884,882
Sikkim	111	212,168	57,756	2,615,358
Daman Diu	100	318,175	86,614	3,922,076
Arunachal Pradesh	89	114,046	31,045	1,405,816
Nagaland	73	97,832	26,632	1,205,949
Mizoram	29	71,022	19,334	875,474
Blank	625	1,248,902	339,976	15,394,965
Total	**1,949,946**	**4,619,381,593**	**1,257,487,844**	**56,942,193,276**

Source: B.R. Shetty, Chairman, UAE Exchange

The remittances through UAE exchange are increasing day by day. The growth of remittances is 15–20 per cent annually. One important reason for the growth is, after recent terrorist attacks most countries have taken various measures to stop money laundering through informal channels. As a result *hundi* is not used to send money as it has become very risky. "A hundi is a written order—usually unconditional—made by one person to another for payment, on demand or after a specified time, of a certain sum of money to a person named therein."[86] Hundis have the same value as money orders or traveller's cheques, so now most of the money is transferred through banks and other remittance houses. The deciding factor is the faster remittance by way of instant cash products such as Xpress money and the enhanced technology like the code banking system. These factors contribute to faster credit through customers' accounts. It is expected that the increase in oil prices will demand more workforce and professionals from India for further development activities in this region. As a result more workforce and professionals from India will come over to this region. So more remittances by Indians are expected to be injected into the Indian economy provided Indian policy makers pay heed to the demands of the Indian diaspora of the UAE.

Following are the various contributions by the Indian diaspora made through the UAE Exchange:[87]

a) Remittance to India in the year 1997: ₹1605 crores
b) Remittance to India in the year 1998: ₹3150 crores
c) Remittance from the UAE Exchange Global Operation in the year 2007: US$ 4.7 billion (₹20,680 crores)
d) Expected remittance for 2008: US$ 6.5 billion (₹27,300 crores)
e) Resurgent India Bond: US$ 120 billion
f) India Millennium Deposit: US$ 500 billion

Emigration acted as a "safety valve" for unemployed Indians in the states of Kerala, Karnataka, Goa, Maharashtra, Gujarat and Punjab. One may critique that the remittances sent in by Indians from thc UAE were ultimately not utilized for the greater good of the nation. A major part of the remittances were used for loan repayments, land and real estate investments, wedding expenses and children's education. In Kerala, major investments were made in real estate resulting in increased land values and boom in the construction sector. The cash inflow also created a demand for cars, refrigerators, television sets, etc., and led to an increase in taxes. The remittances were mainly utilized by middle-class families to improve their standard of living. In Gujarat, the remittances were utilized as working capital by the business-owning families; and in Punjab, it was mainly utilized to migrate to more developed countries.[88] Hence, looking at it from the micro perspective, one can argue against the critiques that these remittances have had a positive impact on the Indian economy at large by increasing the purchasing power and bettering the standard of living at nuclear levels.

During times of crisis such as the Kargil War, Gujarat earthquake, Orissa cyclone, tsunami across the Indian coastline, etc., the maximum support was provided by the Indian diaspora in the UAE. Furthermore, the registered associations of Indians in Dubai, Sharjah, and Abu Dhabi have provided a platform for networking and interaction between the locals and dignitaries coming from India. Various business and professional groups are actively involved in this process. The Business/Professional Group, Abu Dhabi; Overseas Indian Economic Forum, Dubai; Indian Business Council, Dubai; and Indian Sports Clubs have actively been strengthening the bilateral ties between India and UAE by arranging visits for Indian commercial delegates,[89] helping improve the business relations and opportunities between the nations and boosting the foreign exchange reserves.

The amount of foreign exchange sent in by this Indian diaspora is expected to increase further. Recently, the massive infrastructure development projects undertaken by the UAE government and their promotion of Free Zones encouraging foreign investment with a "no tax system" has given an impetus to the Indians to become entrepreneurs and invest in various sectors. As a result, Indians have started investing in various fields, such as real-estate, malls, hotels, manufacturing, retailing, gold, textiles, healthcare, education, etc. Even in these times of economic recession, UAE's economic free zones are attracting many foreign investors. According to Heshem Amiri, Executive Director, Customer Support Service Department (CSSD), Tecom Investment, "Free Zones in general bring a host of benefits including 100 per cent ownerships, exemption of import and export duties or commercial levies, full repatriation of capital and profit and a fifty year tax holiday."[90]

India, being a reservoir of skilled and unskilled manpower, should make appropriate policies to utilize this situation and help further the contributions made by the Indian diaspora in the UAE. Since the Indians in the UAE do not enjoy citizenship rights in the host country their mindset towards India is different than the Indian diasporics in other developed nations. The physical proximity between India and the UAE, improvement of modern communication systems, frequent visits by Indians to their home country has further strengthened their bonds with their homeland.

The contribution of the Indian diaspora towards FDI, however, has not been satisfactory. The amount of FDI in India is only $4 billion whereas China receives $48 billion, half of which is contributed by Chinese expatriates.[91] Most of the interviewees expressed their dissatisfaction towards such shortsightedness among the bureaucrats in India.

The government of India should shoulder some responsibilities too, such as forming a cell for the Indian diaspora in UAE, etc., so that the Indian diaspora and the Indian government can join forces for further betterment.

Expectations of the Indian Diaspora

Each diasporic group in the UAE has different needs and expectations specific to their groups. However, some of their demands are common, summarized as following:

a) The right to be represented in the Indian Parliament
b) NRIs should be given the right to franchise
c) The need of a separate department to deal with diasporic affairs
d) Admission facilities for NRI students. NRI students face various problems regarding admission in schools and professional colleges. Non-fulfilment of domicile requirements impedes the admission process of return migrants.
e) Prevention of bank frauds using FCNR, NRE accounts maintained by the Indian diaspora in the UAE with various Indian banks
f) NRI status identity cards for *bona fide* NRIs in the UAE
g) Reduced consular fees for death registration, prompt issuance of emergency certificates and *tatkal* (emergency) facilities.

The higher-income group of Indians in the UAE, e.g., the professionals and businessmen expect:

a) Preferential business facilities such as duty free import of machinery, equipments, etc., for NRIs trying to set up industries in India
b) Simplification of procedures for trading in equities such as shares, debentures, etc.

Finally, the salaried class suffers from tensions and anxiety related to their jobs. The employment market is suffering from stiff competition. As a result many Indian professionals are migrating to other developed countries such as the UK, the US, Australia, Canada, etc. The worst is faced by the middle- and low-income groups. They expect the respective state governments in India to introduce employment and rehabilitation schemes according to their skills; to include their names in ration cards, electoral rolls, etc. The expatriate workers from Kerala specifically demanded reduction in airfares and introduction of international flights at the Kochi Airport.

Conclusion

The focus of this study has been the contribution of the Indian diaspora and the diasporic Indian entrepreneurs settled in the UAE towards their homeland, India. The above discussion tries to highlight the crucial role that they played in setting up joint ventures, promoting FDIs, facilitating export and mobilizing human resources from India. Their contribution through private transfer, including remittance, has been immense and has helped avert the Balance of Payment crisis. This study wants to draw the attention of the policy makers in India toward this diaspora and diasporic entrepreneurs and the contributions made by them, otherwise not considered as assets worth nurturing. The nature of the Indian diaspora in the UAE differs from those that reside in other parts of the world. The Indian diasporas in other advanced countries have a tendency to spend where they live, settling there permanently, only providing infrequent support to their relatives back home. The Indian diaspora in the UAE, aware of the temporary nature of their stay in the host country, are more eager to invest a major share of their income in their homeland. The Indian diaspora in the UAE can be a source of market information; their expertise can act as a knowledge bridge between two countries. The Indian policy makers should realize the underutilized potentials of its diasporas, especially that of the diasporic entrepreneurs in the UAE, as strategic assets.

This chapter is being concluded with a brief excerpt from the speech given by Sheikh Nahyan bin Mubarak Al Nahyan at the HSBC/FT conference.[92] First, he stated that the brotherly relation between India and UAE had strengthened the ties between the two nations and garnered mutual respect and understanding of each other's interests. He acknowledged that the Indian economy is one of the most vibrant and largest economies, which has a huge consumer market. The other attributes he cited are: a) cost effective manufacturing and service industries; b) sophisticated English-speaking workforce; c) worldwide recognized IT sector; d) strong research and development capabilities; e) sophisticated financial sector and a stable, democratic financial system; f) well established legal and political system with international standards; g) dynamic and visionary leaders. Sheikh Nahyan acknowledged the ingenuity and hard work put in by Indians in the UAE. (And hence, it can be said that the Indian diaspora in the UAE played a great role in creating the "hard working" brand image of India.) He further stated that India should not limit itself to Information Technology and outsourcing and should look at other potential investment opportunities that are prevalent. In the words of Sheikh Nahyan, "We know about Mumbai, Bangalore, and New Delhi. We know about ambitious economic plans for future… but there is a large information gap about the potentials of other states. The knowledge of local culture and business environment of other states will facilitate more investment in India." He also commented on the importance of local culture, expressed very clearly through the remark: "I always make this point by citing to my friends an Arabic saying, 'He who does not know the falcon would roast it'"; falcon is the national bird of UAE. He finally said that there is an urgent need for creation of a centre, which can provide counselling as well as market intelligence to prospective foreign investors. In the UAE, he said, "We have a large group of Indian businessman who provide information informally. In fact my interest in the Indian economy mainly comes from interaction with my Indian friends; but not every person is so fortunate as to have colleagues to provide guidance in their home country."

Based on the above, it may be concluded that the Government of India will have to play a more active role to enhance the bilateral relations between these two nations. The Indian diaspora and the diasporic entrepreneurs can be instrumental in this process; a sense of security and confidence instilled among this diaspora could bring about desired results.

ENDNOTES

1. Paola Grenier, "Social Entrepreneurship: Agency in a Globalizing World," in *Social Entrepreneurship: New Models of Sustainable Social Change*, ed. Alex Nicholls (Oxford, Oxford University Press, 2006), 121.
2. Stanley J. Tambiah, "Transnational Movement, Diaspora, and Multiple Modernities," *Dædalus* 129, no. 1 (Winter 2000): 163.

3. Martin Baumann, "Diaspora, Generalogies of Semantics and Transcultural Comparison," in *Sociology of Diaspora: A Reader*, ed. Ajaya Kumar Sahoo and Brij Maharaj (Jaipur: Rawat Publications, 2007), 63.
4. Roza Tsagarousianou, "Rethinking the Concept of Diaspora: Mobility, Connectivity and Communication in a Globalised World," *Westminister Papers in Communication and Culture* 1, no. 1 (2004): 2.
5. Baumann, "Generalogies of Semantics," 65.
6. Ibid., 65.
7. Judith T. Shuval, "Diaspora Migration: Definitional Ambiguities and a Theoretical Paradigm," in *Sociology of Diaspora: A Reader*, ed. Ajaya Kumar Sahoo and Brij Maharaj (Jaipur: Rawat Publications, 2007), 28.
8. William Safron, "The Jews Diaspora in a comparative and Theoritical Perspectives," in *Sociology of Diaspora: A Reader*, ed. Ajaya Kumar Sahoo and Brij Maharaj (Jaipur: Rawat Publications, 2007), 338.
9. Roza Tsagarouisianou, "Reevaluating Diaspora: Connectivity, Communication and Imagination in a Globalised World," in *The Sociology of Diaspora: A Reader*, ed. Ajaya Kumar Sahoo and Brij Maharaj (Jaipur: Rawat Publications, 2007), 105.
10. Khachig Tölölyan, "The Nation-State and its Others: In Lieu of a Preface," in *Sociology of Diaspora: A Reader*, ed. Ajaya Kumar Sahoo and Brij Maharaj (1991; repr., Jaipur: Rawat Publications, 2007), 23.
11. Gabriel Sheffer, "The Emergence of New Ethno-National Diasporas," in *Sociology of Diaspora: A Reader*, ed. Ajaya Kumar Sahoo and Brij Maharaj (1995; repr., Jaipur: Rawat Publications, 2007), 47.
12. In an interview with Binoy Shetty, dated December 05, 2009.
13. A. Solimino, "Globalising Talent and Human Capital," a paper presented at *Implication for Developing Countries*, ABCDE Conference for Europe, Oslo, 2002.
14. Jagat K. Motwani and others, eds., *The Global Indian Diaspora: Yesterday, Today and Tomorrow* (New York: GOPIO, 1993), 1.
15. Prakash C. Jain, *Indian Labor Migration to the Gulf Countries* (Dubai: Gulf Research Centre, 2006), 10.
16. Myron Weiner, "International Migration and Development: Indians in the Persian Gulf," *Population and Development Review* 8, no. 1 (March 1982): 1–36.
17. Prakash C. Jain, ed., "An 'Incipient' Diaspora: Indians in the Gulf Region," in *Indian Diaspora in West Asia: A Reader* (New Delhi: Manohar Publishers, 2007), 177.
18. K.C. Zachariah, E.T. Mathew and S. Irudaya Rajan, *Dynamics of Migration in Kerala: Determinants, Differentials and Consequences* (New Delhi: Orient Longman, 2003), 222.

19. Source: http://moia.gov.in/writereaddata/pdf/Annual_Report_2008-09.pdf, accessed on April 20, 2010.
20. Abdulla Elamandi, "India's Impact on the Gulf's Economic and Socio-Cultural Life During the British Era," in *Indian Diaspora in West Asia: A Reader*, ed. Prakash C. Jain (New Delhi: Manohar Publishers, 2007), 93.
21. Ibid., 44.
22. Nora Muhammad Al-Qasimi, *The Indian Existence in the Arabian Gulf, 1820–1947* (Sharjah: Department of Education, 2000), 5.
23. Elamandi, "India's Impact on the Gulf," in *Indian Diaspora in West Asia*, 44–5.
24. Jain, "An 'Incipient' Diaspora," 178.
25. Calvin H. Allen Jr., "The Indian Merchants Community of Masqat," in *Indian Diaspora in West Asia: A Reader* (New Delhi: Manohar Publishers, 2007), 60.
26. See the following works: S. Maqbul. Ahmad, *Indo-Arab Relations* (New Delhi: Indian Council for Cultural Relations, 1971); Calvin H. Allen Jr., "Indian Merchant Community of Masqat," *Bullettin of the School of Oriental and African Studies* 44, no. 1 (1981), 39–51; K.N. Chaudhri, *Trade and Civilisation in the Indian Ocean: An Economic History from the Rise of Islam to 1950* (Cambridge: Cambridge University Press, 1986); Robert Lee Franklin, "The Indian Community in Bahrain: Labour Migration in a Plural Society," Ph.D Thesis, Harvard University, Harvard, University Micrifilm International, Ann Arbor; Claude Markovits, *The Global World of Indian Merchants, 1750–1947: Traders of Sind from Bukhara to Panama* (Cambridge: Cambridge University Press, 2000); and, S.B. Miles, *The Countries and Tribes of the Persian Gulf* (London: Frank Cass, 1966).
27. Jain, *Indian Labor Migration*, 10.
28. Markovits, *Global World of Indian Merchants*, 1.
29. *Annual Business Magazine*, Business Monitor International, August 2007.
30. George Fadlo Hourani, *Arab Seafaring: In the Indian Ocean in Ancient and Early Medieval Times*. (Princeton University Press: Princeton, N.J., 1951; Beirut: Khayat, 1963) 91. Citations are to the Khayat edition.
31. Frauke Heard-Bey, *From Trucial States to United Arab Emirates* (1982; repr., London and New York: Longman, 1996), 288.
32. Muhammad Morsy Abdullah, *The United Arab Emirates: A Modern History* (London: Croom Helm; New. York: Barnes and Noble, 1978), 105. Citations are to the Croom Helm edition.
33. Heard-Bey, *From Trucial States*, 134.
34. Ibid., 202.
35. Abdullah, *United Arab Emirates*, 105.

36. Heard-Bey, *From Trucial States*, 133.
37. Miles, *Countries and Tribes*, 468.
38. Fatma Al-Sayegh, "Merchants' Role in a Changing Society: The Case of Dubai, 1900–90," in *Indian Diaspora in West Asia: A Reader*, ed. Prakash C. Jain (New Delhi: Manohar Publishers, 2007), 84.
39. Heard-Bey, *From Trucial States*, 190.
40. Christine E. Dobbin, *Asian Entrepreneurial Minorities: Conjoint Communities in the Making of the World-Economy, 1570–1940* (Oxon: Routledge Curzon, 1996), 3.
41. Source: Bahrain–www.e.gov.bh; Qatar–Government Statistics Authority; Kuwait, Oman and Saudi Arabia–Concerned Indian Embassies; U.A.E–www.uaedirect.com
42. Source: www.uaedirect.com
43. Zachariah and others, *Dynamics of Migration in Kerala*, 148.
44. Roger Ballard, "The South Asian Presence in Britain and its Transnational Connections," in *Sociology of Diaspora: A Reader*, eds. Ajaya Kumar Sahoo and Brij Maharaj (Jaipur: Rawat Publication, 2007), 600.
45. P.V. Vivekanand, *Pearl of Dubai* (Dubai: Quality Printing Service, 2008), 15.
46. Vasanti Sundaram, *Footprints: Memoirs of an Indian Patriarch* (Dubai: Motivate Publishing, 2009), 64.
47. Vivekanand, *Pearl of Dubai*, 12
48. Marcovits, *Global World of Indian Merchants*, 25.
49. Ibid., 36.
50. Sundaram, *Footprints*, 65.
51. In an interview with Mohan Jashanmal, dated May 15, 2010.
52. Sundaram, *Footprints*, 67.
53. Rosemarie Said Zahlan, *The Making of the Modern Gulf States: Kuwait, Bahrain, Qatar, the United Arab Emirates, and Oman* (London: Unwin Hyman Ltd, 1989), 20.
54. Sundaram, *Footprints*, 69–70.
55. Pancholia, as cited by Vivekanand, *Pearl of Dubai*, 18.
56. Sundaram, *Footprints*, 87.
57. Pancholia, as cited by Vivekanand, *Pearl of Dubai*, 19.
58. Al-Sayegh, "Changing Society," 85.
59. Abu Dhabi Marine Operating Company (ADMA-OPCO), *A Sucessful Journey through time, 1962–2007* (Abu Dhabi: ADMA-OPCO, 2007) 19.
60. James Onley, *The Arabian Frontier of the British Raj: Merchants, Rulers and the British in the Nineteenth Century Gulf* (New York: Oxford University Press, 2007), vii, 3–4.
61. *Ibid.*, vii.
62. *Ibid.*, 3.

63. *Ibid.*, 3
64. Onley, *Arabian Frontier*, 33.
65. *Ibid.*, 4.
66. *Ibid.*, 103.
67. *Ibid.*
68. *Ibid.*
69. Heard-Bey, *From Trucial States*, 190.
70. Source: Present Value of Trade Embassy Paper (DGCIS), Indian Embassy.
71. Onley, *Arabian Frontier of the British Raj*, vii.
72. *Ibid*, 102.
73. Source: Qatar-Government statistics authority, Kuwait, Oman, Saudi Arabia, Concerned Indian embassies—www.uaedirect.com (UAE); www.e.gov.bh (Bahrain).
74. Source: www.uaedirect.com
75. Source: www.uaedirect.com
76. Weiner, Myron. "International Migration and Development: Indians in the Persian Gulf." *Population and Development Review* 8, no. 1 (March 1982): 1–36.
77. Source: www.uaedirect.com; Courtesy: Indian Embassy in the UAE.
78. Zachariah and others, *Dynamics of Migration in Kerala*, 50.
79. Jain, "An 'Incipient'Diaspora," 182.
80. K.C. Zachariah, K.P. Kannan and S. Irudaya Rajan, eds., *Kerala's Gulf Connection: CDS Studies on International Labour Migration from Kerala State in India* (Thiruvananthapuram: Center for Development Studies, 2002), 162.
81. *Gulf News*, Friday, January 29, 2010.
82. Jain, *Indian Diaspora in West Asia*, 182.
83. In an interview with M. Chauhan, Manager, Bank of Baroda, Abu Dhabi branch, Abu Dhabi, July 26, 2008.
84. Data provided by Bank of Baroda, Abu Dhabi branch.
85. Source: Indian Embassy, Commercial Division, Abu Dhabi, UAE.
86. Scotts Cameron Levi, *The Indian Diaspora in Central Asia and its Trade: 1550–1900*. (Leiden; Boston; Köln: Brill, 2002), 203.
87. Courtesy: B.R. Shetty, Chairman, UAE Exchange.
88. Weiner, "International Migration," 133.
89. In an interview with Talmiz Ahmed, dated July 30, 2008.
90. *Gulf News*, Special Report on Magazine Free Zones, March 15, 2010.
91. Anand Mullo, *Voices of the Indian Diaspora* (Delhi: Motilal Banarsidass, 2007), 42.
92. Doing Business in India the Next Wave, a conference held in Abu Dhabi, on Wednesday, October 7, 2009.

5

Indian Entrepreneurs in the UAE

The Indian diasporic entrepreneurs in the UAE have received a lot less attention and recognition than they deserve despite of their contributions towards both countries. Whenever talks regarding the recent growth of India occur, a lot of credit is given to the politicians back home, however, the role played by the overseas Indian entrepreneurs, especially the ones in the UAE, is rarely mentioned. Prakash C. Jain commented: "It's a pity that we hardly have any information on Indian entrepreneurship in the Gulf Countries."[1]

In order to understand various aspects of entrepreneurship, it is necessary to define what it entails. The true definition of the terms "entrepreneur" and "entrepreneurship" has been debated upon a lot. Various schools of thought have defined it in their own terms. The review of literature given in the first chapter of this study also represents this diversity in defining an entrepreneur.

According to Kilby, the search for an entrepreneur can be compared to an episode in the famous children's story *Winnie the Pooh*.[2] Kilby stated: "The Heffalump is a rather large and very important animal. He has been hunted by many individuals using various ingenious trapping devices, but no one so far has succeeded in capturing him. All who claim to have caught sight of him report that he is enormous, but they disagree in his particularities. Not having explored his current habitat with sufficient care, some hunters have used as bait their own favourite dishes and have then tried to persuade people that what they caught was a Heffalump. However, very few are convinced and the search goes on."[3]

The true concept of entrepreneur is just such an elusive one. As entrepreneurs and entrepreneurship are a major part of this study, an attempt is made to synthesize the definitions presented by different authors/schools.

The French School: Richard Cantillion, a French banker, first used the term "entrepreneur" in economic theory. He used the term to refer to the dealers "who buy the wares of the country…, give for them a fixed price to sell them again wholesale and retail at uncertain prices."[4] Entrepreneurs are risk bearers and must make decisions during times of uncertainty. Jean Baptiste described an entrepreneur as a person who possesses various skills to start an economic unit. According to him, an entrepreneur possesses "…judgment, perseverance and a knowledge of the world as well as business. He is called upon to estimate, with tolerable accuracy, the importance of the specific product, the probable amount of the demand and the means of its production: at one time, he must employ a great number of hands; at another, buy or order the raw material, collect labourers, find consumers, and give at all times a rigid attention to order and economy; in a word he must possess the art of superintendence and administration."[5]

The British School: In his seminal work *Wealth of Nations*, Adam Smith described the entrepreneur as an individual with unusual foresight whose commercial objective motivates him to establish an organization. Profit is the reward for taking risks. However, Adam Smith failed to distinguish the role of a capitalist from that of an entrepreneur.

John Stuart Mill, a British economist, opined that an entrepreneur is the founder of a business, and whose necessary attributes are intelligence, knowledge and trustworthiness. According to Mill, every person does not possess the intelligence and capabilities needed to run an industrial enterprise. He believed that education plays a great role in cultivating and improving these attributes.

According to Marshall, anxieties, mental strain and risks are part of management functions. The entrepreneur must be innovative but alert. Profits are his reward. However, Marshall was criticized for his inability to communicate the true implication of the concept.[6]

The German School: The main question raised by the German school of thought was how to compensate the entrepreneur for his talent. The representatives of the German school then opined that it is the entrepreneur who takes uninsurable risk and carries whole problems home. Therefore, according to them, the entrepreneur is the risk taker, innovator and problem-solver, and, unlike the returns going to a capitalist, the profit is the leftover needed by the entrepreneur to shoulder the uninsurable risk and the incentive to keep innovating.[7]

The Austrian School: Karl Menger, the originator of the Austrian school of thought, described entrepreneurs as change agents who transform resources into goods and services beneficial to the consumer. According to him, entrepreneurs gather information about the economic situation and bring economic changes on the basis of their awareness and proper assessment of the situation. Entrepreneurs play a key role in industrial development by acquiring a proper understanding of one economic condition in one country. According to him, risk bearing is not an essential function of an entrepreneur.[8]

Joseph Schumpeter is called the father of entrepreneurial theory. He conceived of the entrepreneur as an innovator who brings about changes in the existing production process or introduces a new process or product. Thus the entrepreneur with his innovation reduces the cost of production and increases profit. Schumpeter's "new production function" has a broader concept which includes:

i) The introduction of a new good or a new quality of goods.
ii) The development of a new method of production or new way of commercially handling a commodity.
iii) The opening of a new market.
iv) Capitalization of a new source of supply of raw materials or half-manufactured goods.
v) Establishing a new organization or a new industry.[9]

It has been criticized that Schumpeter was only concerned with a higher level of entrepreneurship. He suggested very little for the lower/inferior levels of entrepreneurship. "Von Mises felt that Schumpeter has confused entrepreneurial activity with technological innovation."[10]

Despite the criticisms levelled against him, this study acknowledges Schumpeter for providing the entrepreneur with a significant position in the economy. A proper analysis of the time and the milieu in which Schumpeter wrote his *Theory of Economic Development* can support this statement.

Theory of Economic Development was first published in 1912 in Schumpeter's native language, Austrian. He commented that in a static economy neither profit nor interest is feasible, and it is the function of the entrepreneur to bring about dynamism in the economy through innovation. At that time the American economy was dominated by giant monopolistic corporations. The role of the "individual entrepreneur" got blurred due to the domination of collective entrepreneurs at the corporate-level decision-making process. When Schumpeter joined Harvard University as a professor he came in contact with many other scholars. One of them was Arthur H. Cole, with whom he co-founded the Research Centre in Entrepreneurial History at Harvard in 1948. Cole modified the Schumpeterian model to a certain extent. According to him, entrepreneurial functions are similar to managerial functions and thus the individual received little recognition in Cole's analysis. Cole's "purposeful activity" is similar to Schumpeter's "creative response". When he emigrated to America, Schumpeter recognized the rise of collective entrepreneurship. He explained the reason as: "Technological progress is increasingly becoming the business of the teams of trained specialists who turn out what is required and make it work in a predictable way."[11]

The difference between Cole and Schumpeter is in their emphasis. On the basis of the above discussion, this study avers that entrepreneurial activities may encompass the actions of a single person as an agent of the firm in the economy as well as the collective entrepreneurship of larger companies.

In the words of Chell, Haworth and Brearley, "Schumpeter is the 'architect of a theory of economic development' in which the entrepreneur is central; the entrepreneur's role is to disturb the economy's status quo through innovation."[12]

The American School: Francis A. Walker was perhaps the first major representative of the American school. He believed exceptional abilities and opportunities are the two fundamental requirements for a successful business. He believed that entrepreneurial functions were different from those performed by capitalists. He classified entrepreneurship into four categories: the rare; the gifted; the high order of talented entrepreneurs; and the ne'er-do-well type. His theory took into consideration the psychological characteristics of entrepreneurship. To him, profit is the return against entrepreneurship skills and ability.[13]

Fredrick B. Hawley and John R. Common, notable American economists, also supported Walker's view. According to Tripathi, "[i]t was John Bates Clark, however, who conceived of a direct link between entrepreneurial profit and successful introduction into the economic process of technological, commercial or organizational improvement."[14] According to Clark, innovation is the major aspect of entrepreneurial function.

Contemporary Theories on Entrepreneurship

G.L.S. Shackle, Israel Kirzner, Mark Casson and T.W. Schultz are notable exponents of the idea of psychological aspects being used in analysing the entrepreneurial behaviour.

According to Israel Kirzner, the entrepreneurial function is "to notice what others have overlooked". Distinguishing an arbitrageur from the entrepreneur he commented that the entrepreneur tackles uncertainty with creative imagination and alertness, whereas an arbitrager adjusts price and cost based on experience.

Casson stated that the entrepreneur is a person whose judgments differ from others. Based on this judgment the decisions he makes are what guides the team and optimally allocates the scarce resources. He further argued that successful entrepreneurs are those who have other valuable attributes like imagination and foresight. He also believed that these qualities could be enhanced with experience and training.

Sultz, a pioneer of human capital theory, broadened the idea of entrepreneurship. He opined that risk-bearing capacity is not the only essential attribute of an entrepreneur. Entrepreneurial ability is the "ability to reallocate their services in response to changes in the value of the work they do."[15] He stressed the role of education in enhancing the power of perception which places the entrepreneur in an advantageous position.

Herbert and Link defined the entrepreneur as, "...someone who specializes in taking responsibilities for making judgmental decisions and affect the location, the form and the use of goods, resources or institutions."[16]

Psychological and Sociological Theories

The entrepreneur's contribution to society is immense and is acknowledged across societies all over the world. Such importance has prompted researchers to take into consideration the sociological and psychological aspects related to entrepreneurship. Psycho-sociological theorists have advocated that the personalities, traits, skills and attitudes of entrepreneurs and their environmental responsibilities play a key role towards their growth.

The most renowned proponent of the psychological theory was David McClelland, who stated that entrepreneurs are different from others from the standpoint of traits and motivation. They are guided by their strong motivation towards achievement. They are "high achievers"; they love challenging situations and shoulder various types of responsibilities without hesitation. He advocated that this achievement-oriented motivation can be developed through a keen training and socialization process. Davidsson supported this theory by emphasizing the role of achievement-oriented motivation for the growth and betterment of entrepreneurship.[17]

Studying the varied literature on entrepreneurship, Thomas Begley and David P. Boyd have identified the following five characteristics of entrepreneurs:[18]

1) ***Need Achievement*:** Entrepreneurs are high in McClelland's concept of need achievement.
2) ***Internal Locus of Control*:** Individuals who control their own life. Luck and fate has no role to play in their lives.
3) ***Tolerance for risk*:** Entrepreneurs who are moderate risks taker can expect they can get higher return than those who take higher risk or no risk at all.
4) ***Tolerance for ambiguity*:** Entrepreneurs have to face ambiguity as they take initiative to do something for the first time and taking such risks is their livelihood.
5) ***"Type A" behaviour*:** This type of personality motivates the entrepreneur to get more within limited period.

Sociological theorists have also explained the agency of entrepreneurship from a sociological standpoint. According to them the success of an entrepreneur depends largely on environmental factors rather than his skill. They have emphasized that the main factor behind becoming an entrepreneur is their respective sociological backgrounds.[19]

Defining the Entrepreneur

Synthesizing the ideas gathered from the above stated concepts, the entrepreneur may be defined as a person endowed with farsightedness, an impeccable judgment, highly driven and with a knack for creative thinking, who starts an enterprise with a profit motive, locates, coordinates and mobilizes resources for an economic activity, makes the most of opportunities available in the market, organizes and manages an enterprise with the right decisions amidst various risks. In a sense, he is an alchemist.

An entrepreneur is a risk taker who runs a business for profit and growth. His behaviour is based on innovation and risk taking and the employment of strategic management principles. Joseph A. Schumpeter was amongst the first to identify the entrepreneur as an important entity in the economic structure. He defined an entrepreneur as an individual who carries "new combinations to the means of production". An entrepreneur is characterized by creative activity which is manifested by innovation. This creative activity is used to generate profit. Several studies have focused on the various personality traits of an entrepreneur. In the words of Schumpeter, "The entrepreneur in an advanced economy is an individual who introduces something new in economy—a method of production not yet tested by experience in the branch of manufacture concerned, a product with which consumers are not yet familiar, a new source of raw material or of new markets and the like."[20] The role of an entrepreneur is that of an economic agent who organizes, supervises and coordinates the various factors of production, to manufacture and sell the product, and make profit.

If the five categories of behaviour characteristics of an entrepreneur categorized by Schumpeter are to be applied, the study speculates the occurrence of the following:

(a) Introduction of new goods
(b) Introduction of new methods
(c) Creating new markets
(d) Finding new resources and establishing new supply chains
(e) Industrial re-organization.

If a minimum of four of the above criteria is observed in a given firm, it can be termed an entrepreneurial venture. The Indian entrepreneurs in the UAE have been found to act upon all of the above listed criteria.

To summarize, an individual can be defined as an entrepreneur if he brings various resources together for the initiation of a venture. An entrepreneur is considered a success if his enterprise(s) survives beyond two years.[21]

Indian Entrepreneurs in the UAE

UAE entrepreneurs can be categorized into three broad groups: pre-oil; post-oil; and new-generation entrepreneurs. The conditions in the pre-oil era were markedly different than those in the present era. An insight into the various environmental factors that have been affecting them across time would be useful. A brief account of their struggle in the UAE (mostly received through oral interviews) will help to comprehend the sufferings faced by Indian entrepreneurs in the past and now.

***Pre-Oil Generation of Indian Entrepreneurs*:** In the pre-oil era, Indian entrepreneurs had to struggle with unfavourable living conditions—lack of electricity, poor infrastructure and inadequate housing—which prevented them from bringing along their families from India. Alienation from their families had a great psychological impact on them amidst already rough living conditions. Proper roads were not there then, nor many cars suitable for the desert. Owning a car was not an option as there was no police department or any governing body issuing driving licenses. Only ex-service army trucks and four-wheel drives such as Land Rovers were used for human and goods transport. The drivers were mostly locals and Bedouins, people who were familiar with the desert tracks. Vehicles used to follow the tracks previously created by the army vehicles.

People used to carry a shovel and a sheet of iron in their vehicle at all times, for emergencies such as breakdown and sand-trapped tyres. Travelling at night was a risky business as there was no lighting to guide cars through the non-motorable roads. There were no petrol pumps either; people used to fill their petrol tanks by siphoning oil from huge oil-barrels stored in shops. Until the 1950s, camels were practically the main mode of travelling between Abu Dhabi and Dubai and each trip used to take three to four days.[22] The only exceptions were the sea-routes, such as the way to the northern Emirates. Several lives were lost to dehydration while stranded in the middle of the desert through transportation failure. Mohammed Fahim, the first Vice President of the Chamber of Commerce, lost his sister due to the tragic delay in medical attention caused by inadequate transportation facilities.[23]

Difficulties with irrigation and water transport were a few among many other causes for concern amongst the newly arrived entrepreneurs from India. Communication with families and business units back home was very difficult because there was no post office until 1958. The vegetarian Banias could not adapt to the local diet of poultry and cattle, and suffered from malnutrition. Dates were the only edibles available to them in this desert climate where cultivating vegetables and fruit plantations was not possible. By and large, they had to import their food from India. Despite all the physical hardships, the Indian entrepreneurs found a sense of support and mutual understanding among the local population as they worked together towards creating a better life in the UAE.

Business in those days was largely based on trust and word-of-honour; no receipts were maintained against any payments made between two business parties, balances were maintained and settled verbally. According to Ram Buxani, "It was ITL, our company in Dubai that introduced the system of receipts against payment made."[24]

During the 1960s, India contributed immensely to the fast developing businesses in the UAE such as textiles and consumer goods. Dubai became the transit point for the fabrics that were to be delivered from other countries to the rest of the subcontinent. The foundation of the relationship between the two countries was based on mutual benefit and trust that stood the test of time.[25]

***Post-Oil Generation of Indian Entrepreneurs*:** With the discovery of oil, the scenario started changing. It brought along with it a boom in the economy of the Trucial States. According to Rosemarie Said Zahlan, "The States whose rulers had signed the Perpetual Maritime Truce become known as Trucial States, a name which persisted until 1971 when they united to form the federation known as the United Arab Emirates. The "States of Trucial Oman", the "Trucial States", and the "Trucial Coast" were [names] used interchangeably and in a seemingly haphazard manner.[26] The Perpetual Maritime Truce was signed between Britain and the various Sheikhs of this region with an intention to stop the hostilities at sea. The presence of various international oil companies and the influx of foreign workers working in the developmental activities in this region created a sudden demand for food and household goods, opening up a niche market for entrepreneurs. The Indian entrepreneurs seized this opportunity for business and contributed a lot to the UAE society by meeting their demands. The massive economic growth of the UAE compared to its GCC (Gulf Cooperation Council) counterparts can be attributed to its non-oil economic policy. This diversification introduced by the farsighted leaders of UAE boosted the growth potential of this country much ahead of the other neighbouring West Asian and North-east African countries. Abu Dhabi's non-oil sector contributed 175 billion Dirhams to the GDP in 2009 ($1 = 3.67 AED). Major growth were seen in the manufacturing sector at 9.2 per cent, the construction sector at 18 per cent, real estate at 15 per cent, the banking sector at 12 per cent and the hospitality industry at 15 per cent.[27]

Despite the success with diversification, oil and natural gas reserves remain the major source of income and revenue generation for the UAE economy. The UAE has merely 97.8 billion cubic meters of proven oil reserves, about 9.8 per cent of the total proven world oil resource. It has also 6073 billion cubic meters of proven natural gas reserves, approximately 4.6 per cent of the total proven world natural gas reserve. Ninety five per cent of UAE's total gas reserves are located in Abu Dhabi. Recently some Indian Companies have successfully penetrated the UAE economy: Punj Lloyd, who have been actively involved in oil and gas sector; and Larsen and Toubro, in power as well as oil and gas sectors.[28]

The UAE government is expected to spend more than 80 billion Dirhams in the next five years. The government is embarking on various developmental projects in the tourism sector. There have been various expansions in local airlines programs such as Gulf Air, Emirates Airlines, Etihad and Air Arabia. Emirates Airlines stunned the industry with an order for thirty two Airbus A380 planes worth $11.5 billion. The airlines signed this deal with Airbus at the Berlin Air show. With this record deal in aviation, Emirates has repositioned Dubai as a gateway to worldwide travel.[29] These airlines are also providing various packages to attract more tourists to this region. The Burj Al Arab in Dubai, is one of the world's finest hotels and tallest buildings, with 60 floors and 202 rooms. Besides, Sadiyat Island, in Abu Dhabi, is yet another example of the boom in tertiary sector in the UAE.[30]

The extremities in climate, however, have not deterred the UAE government from investing in the agricultural sector. There are 40 million date palms in the UAE. The country is striving towards self-sufficiency with its own supply of food grains. The Khalifa International Date Palm Award (KIDPA) with a value of AED 2 million, attracts a large number of participants from around the world each year. ATUL Limited, a leading chemical company owned by an Indian entrepreneur received the prestigious KIDPA for the year 2009, and was honoured with first prize in the category of "Distinguished Procedure" among participants from eighteen other countries.[31] The Indian entrepreneurs in the UAE can be important agents who can help bank major economic opportunities developing in the UAE if adequately backed by the Indian government.

The diversification policy allowed the UAE government to shield its economy from fluctuations in oil prices.[32] The reasons behind the success of this diversification policy are as follows:

(a) Open trade regime.
(b) No legal restriction on capital outflow.
(c) Competitive business environment.
(d) Low taxes.
(e) Well developed infrastructure with all modern facilities.

Thus the prudent policy-makers of the UAE transformed a rural- and trade-based economy into a modern one and introduced the UAE to the global scene.[33] By joining the GCC, the UAE became a part of a larger, common market. A favourable business environment coupled with the openness to trade and trade facilitation enabled the UAE to attract more Foreign Direct Investment (FDI). The opening up of the gas market, tourism, construction, financial services and high technology industry has further increased the confidence of investors.

The political structure of the UAE federation is unique. It provides freedom to the independent States to freely pursue their own economic policies. As a result each State is in a position to utilize its capabilities according to its potential. For example, Abu Dhabi (capital of the UAE) traditionally focuses on petrochemical and fertilizer production and has recently diversified towards construction and tourism. The Abu Dhabi government took an initiative in January 2006 to develop a new port at Taweelah, situated between Abu Dhabi and Dubai. The port was named Khalifa Port. This eight-billion-AED project was essential to enhancing business opportunities in tourism and industry. In order to attract more FDI, the Abu Dhabi government has passed a new law allowing for hundred- per cent ownership rights in the industrial city in three sectors.[34]

Dubai is the most "business friendly" location amongst all the Emirates. It has always focused on entrepôt trade, tourism and finance. The success of Dubai can be attributed towards its lenient business investment policy. An efficiently functioning port, good airport facilities, and infrastructure contributed further towards this process. The benefits of trading in Dubai are:[35]

a) Reduced transaction costs in trade.
b) Easier custom clearance.
c) Greater export market.

Free Trade Zones

The massive growth in the service sector has prompted the launch of Free Trade Zones (FTZ) for media, knowledge and technology services. The UAE government has developed 32 free trade zones. At present, 5000 companies with an approximate investment of $4 billion are operating in these areas. The most successful free zones are Jebel Ali and Jafza. Nearly 80 countries are operating in Jafza. The main attractions of these free zones are as follows:

1. 100 per cent ownership by foreign companies.
2. Full import and export tax exemption.
3. Exemption of commercial levies.
4. Full repatriation of capital and profit.
5. Long term (multi-year) leases.
6. Easy access to the sea and airport.
7. Energy connection (often at subsidized prices).
8. Proper guidance in labour recruitment.
9. Various kinds of support services.

All these favourable incentives attract new companies to these areas. Recent major companies in India are planning to shift their head offices to Dubai.[36]

In short, it can be stated that these FTZs have played a key role in increasing the non-hydrocarbon export. A tax-free environment combined with other benefits such as no restriction on foreign ownership and freedom to repatriate the capital and profit have attracted many companies to set up operations in these FTZs. These FTZs also operate as major distribution centres, providing storage and warehousing facilities. Currently, most of the companies here are engaged in assembling electrical products, light engineering and manufacturing.[37]

Dubai Internet City

FTZs, the industrial muscle of the UAE economy, were able to attract many global information and communication technology (ICT) companies such as Microsoft, Oracle, Sony, Ericsson and HP, as well as Indian companies, to the Dubai Internet City (DIC). The state-of-the-art technology base at the DIC provides cost-effective Business Process Outsourcing (BPO) facilities to these companies. The ICT cluster at the DIC provides high-quality networking facilities among many other business utilities, resulting in better enhanced knowledge-sharing and problem-solving capabilities. It is the biggest IT infrastructure facility in West Asia. However, the FTZs, the DIC in particular, primarily depend on an expatriate workforce. It has been criticized that the UAE tax havens could not generate many job opportunities for UAE nationals. But compared to the FTZs, many nationals are engaged in the IT sector in the UAE.

Sharjah has focused on tourism and small- and medium-scale manufacturing centres as its economic strengths. Ras Al Khaimah specializes in cement production and pharmaceuticals. The northern Emirates, besides being popular tourist spots owing to their scenic beauty and climate, have also been developing their shipping, agriculture, mining and quarrying industries.

Labour and Employment-Related Information

The knowledge of all existing Labour and Employment laws of the UAE will be of immense value to those who wish to invest, do business or work in the UAE. In the following passage the study will highlight some such legal/national policies the knowledge of which, the study believes, will help those willing with calculating their benefits and risks. The UAE government has recently taken measures to implement its Emiritization policies. This is to check the growing imbalance between the UAE nationals and the émigrés. The UAE nationals are under the threat of becoming a minority against the 98-percent-strong expatriate/non-UAE workforce in the private sector. To bring this imbalance under control various steps have been taken by the UAE government. To increase the number of UAE nationals in the workforce of the economy, the government has been encouraging the private sector to conduct various training programmes involving UAE nationals to ensure that they are integrated into the workforce as swiftly as possible. The government has also introduced special employment quotas for UAE nationals in the public sector, e.g., oil and gas, banking and telecommunication, etc. These divisions are taking various measures to provide the nationals with working positions in the UAE economy. Etisalat has successfully introduced various recruiting and training programmes for UAE nationals. There is no law granting the "right to organize and bargain collectively" in the UAE, however, the UAE government does not prohibit workers from engaging in collective bargaining. The ministerial resolution no. 307, of 2003, stipulates that "masters and workers have to solve their collective disputes through direct negotiations, reconciliations and then arbitration according to the procedure mentioned in this resolution".[38] Recently, workers have been demonstrating peacefully outside the Ministry of Labour to address their grievances regarding non-payment of their wages.

The UAE government has been revising its labour laws regarding creation of labour unions or associations. In the FTZs, each company deals with its labour disputes through their own labour department, which are outside the direct control of UAE's Ministry of Labour. Also, work permits are restricted to people above the age of 18 years. Normal working hours in the UAE are 8 hours a day, 6 days a week. There is no minimum-wage law and the compensation packages are aligned with market demand and supply.[39] However, each of the labour contracts are reviewed by the Ministry of Labour and if any of the proposed wages is found to be unacceptable, it does not get sanctioned. Although, what is deemed as "acceptable" is disputable as there is no minimum wage set. Humane laws, such as work-exemption during the heat-hours in the afternoons, from 12:30 hrs to 15:00 hrs (UAE Standard Time), through the months of July and August, have been implemented.[40] Also, the World Bank surveys have found that compared to other countries the UAE is more flexible with its laws regarding hiring and firing workers.[41]

Legal System in the UAE

A) Laws Governing Foreign Investments in the UAE

The code-of-conduct for business establishments in the UAE are governed by both federal and State authorities. There are four major laws governing foreign investments in the UAE:[42]

1. The Federal Company Law
2. The Commercial Agencies Law
3. Federal Industry Law
4. Government Tender Law

1. *The Federal Company Law:* All foreign companies established in the UAE and their branch offices come under the jurisdiction of the Federal Company Law. According to this law, foreign investors are allowed to own a maximum of 49 per cent of the business while a minimum 51 per cent is owned by a UAE-national partner. The offshore branch offices are also required to have a national agent. All general

partnership interests must be co-owned by a UAE national. In the case of limited liability companies, the foreign shareholders are entitled to hold a maximum aggregate 49 per cent stake.[43] In 2006 there was an amendment to the ownership laws for insurance companies. The new law stated that 75 to 100 per cent must be owned by a UAE national or a UAE corporation.[44] However, the Dubai government has opened a number of strategic economic sectors facilitating foreign investment. "This law now allows up to 100 per cent ownership in some strategic economic sectors with big investments and high technology as that adds values to the economy."[45]

2. *The Commercial Agencies Law*: This law requires foreign principals to distribute their products in the UAE only through exclusive commercial agents who are UAE nationals or companies wholly owned by UAE nationals. On June 18, 2006, the UAE government made the following amendments to the Commercial Agencies Law:[46]

a) Mutual agreement between partners is mandatory for renewal of agency agreement.
b) Contracts were limited to a fixed time period.
c) Both parties were given the right to file a suit for damages.
d) Approval is no longer required for "liberalized goods".

3. *Federal Industry Law*: According to this law, 51 per cent ownership of any industrial project needs to be held by a UAE national. The law also stipulates the project has to be overseen by a UAE national or a board of directors consisting of UAE nationals. The oil companies, however, were exempted from the Industry Law. Small capital investment projects, governed under special laws or agreements, were exempted too.[47]

4. *Government Tender Law*: Foreign companies who wish to bid for a federal project must enter into a joint venture or an agency arrangement with a UAE national or company.

B) Property Laws in the UAE

The UAE regulatory and legal framework is still evolving. Non-UAE nationals—expatriates, foreign individual investors and foreign owned corporations—are not entitled to freehold or own property outside of the prescribed or designated areas. Real estate comes under federal jurisdiction of the UAE but an Emirate national is permitted to seek redressal under local laws.

1. *Property Law in Abu Dhabi*: Property Law no. 19, effective since 2005, allows only UAE nationals to have freehold titles to land within Abu Dhabi. GCC nationals are permitted to own the freehold of land in select areas in Abu Dhabi listed under investment zones by the Abu Dhabi government. Recently Sheikh Khalifa bin Zayed Al Nahyan made an amendment to this law in February 2007, thereafter allowing non-UAE nationals to own properties excluding the land, i.e., they can own office buildings, factories and apartments within the investment zones, but not the land that the property stands on. Such right to ownership is not like a freehold title in the traditional sense of land ownership. The owner of the property leases the land from its owner and builds upon it. The law permits non-UAE nationals to have up to a 99-year renewable lease.[48]

2. *Property Law in Dubai*: Property Law no. 7, effective since 2006, states that non-UAE nationals are only permitted to hold an interest over land situated within the areas listed by the Dubai government as lands that can be owned by non-UAE nationals. There are currently 30 such designated areas in Dubai.[49]

3. *Property Law in Sharjah*: In places like Sharjah that are governed by the ruler of the area, non-UAE nationals are allowed to own properties under a 25-year renewable leasehold contract only with the consent of the ruler.[50]

With the rise in the investment trend in the UAE, it is expected that the UAE government will modify its property laws to further the confidence amongst the foreign investors.

C) Laws Governing Intellectual Property Rights

The UAE government has taken various measures to attract foreign investors. A favourable change has occurred in the system of law governing intellectual property rights in the UAE. Such rights are protected here by three main laws:[51]

1) The Trademark Laws, administered by the Ministry of Economy and Commerce.
2) The Copyright Law, administered by the Ministry of Information and Culture.
3) The Patent and Design Law, administered by Finance and Industry.

The copyright law was enacted in July 2002. The UAE is recognized as a regional leader in computer software piracy control.

D) Funds Transfer Policy

Other than Israeli currency, restrictions have been imposed by the UAE government on import or export of AED (United Arab Emirates Dirham) and foreign currencies. Investors, however, do not face any delay in the exchange process. But regarding high-value money transfers, there are strict requirements for documentation. After an attack in September 2001, the UAE government put in place the Anti-Money Laundering Legislation Act by the end of 2001, which follows stringent reporting requirements for any wire transfers exceeding $545, and currency importation reporting requirements for amounts exceeding $10,800. Banks and other financial institutions also have to report to the Central Bank of the UAE if any transaction exceeds $54,000. Any violation is punishable with up to seven years imprisonment.[52]

The various amendments of these laws reflect the UAE's intention to maintain its position as a global trade partner. There are many other laws that come into play when one considers setting up a business in the UAE. From January 1, 2003, the UAE has implemented an import tariff of 5 per cent on most goods, whereas there is a 50 per cent tariff on alcohol, and a 100 per cent tariff on tobacco. Fifty-three foods and agricultural goods were exempted from this tariff.[53] There is no income or consumption tax in the UAE, however, foreign banks pay a 20 per cent tax on their profits and foreign oil companies with equity pay taxes and royalties on their proceeds.

Back in the pre-oil era, trade licenses were not required by investors when setting up a business. However now, no business can be carried out by a UAE resident in a Free Trade Zone unless they have a relevant license to do so.

A point that can be considered as a weakness of the UAE economy is that the Dirham is pegged to the US dollar. As a result, the UAE government has minimal control over the monetary policies needed to tackle inflationary pressures.[54] Although relatively a peaceful country that steers clear of any controversy, the UAE is nonetheless located in a volatile region at present, and the increased risk profile may affect investors' decisions.

Also the court and civil proceedings here are conducted in a manner that may cause difficulties to a foreign entity. One can easily appear in court with no legal representation; however, all court proceedings here are conducted in Arabic, even written evidence must be produced in Arabic. Also, only lawyers of UAE nationality are permitted the right to audience before the court. Foreign judgments are not entertained in Dubai.

E) Immigration Policy

The presence of a large working population of expatriate workers in the UAE has led to the marginalization of UAE nationals in all sectors of work. A common opinion amongst the UAE nationals and other GCC countries about the UAE losing its identity as a result of this massive influx of foreign workers is what led to the formulation of UAE immigration policy. According to the UAE Labour Report 2000, other major problems besides the demographic imbalance are the increasing numbers of foreign workers, and the UAE's dependence on unskilled workers. An initiative was taken to decrease this imbalance by reducing the quota of visa permits usually given to South Asian unskilled workers, as they form about one-third of the population. Also the cost of hiring and importing unskilled manual workers has been increased by the government to lessen their appointment. The deployment of modern technology is being encouraged instead. A minimum high-school certificate has also been made mandatory for an unskilled worker to qualify for a work visa.

The ability to organize, calculate and speculate properly is what distinguishes a good merchant. And that is how the Indian businessmen-turned-entrepreneurs in the UAE were able to secure themselves a superior position in UAE society compared to other nationalities. The joint-family structure prevalent amongst these Indian communities played an important role, providing them with the much needed psychological and monetary support to take their ventures into new worlds. Recently, a few prominent Keralites have also positioned themselves well in the UAE market. The trust that these Indian business communities were able to generate in the UAE played a key role in positioning themselves in that society. The trust had to be strong enough, particularly in the olden days, because business transactions in UAE were conducted without any written paperwork.[55]

Field interviews revealed how they mobilized their resources with alertness and timeliness to set up a firm ground for their businesses. An exemplary use of opportunity can be cited in the initiative taken by B.R. Shetty, Director of the New Medical Hospital, to quickly set up specialized swine flu medical units in the UAE at the earliest reports of the outbreak of the potential pandemic. Their alternative business skills have enabled them to find new markets and opportunities, and their global mindset has prompted them to initiate various ventures. International entrepreneurship is defined as a combination of innovation, proactive and risk taking behaviours that crosses national borders and creates value within an organization.[56] Thus their capacity to adapt themselves to changing conditions while creating opportunities from nothing has been crucial. According to Maria Aggestam and James J. Keenan, entrepreneurs are like "vaults, that is, containers, stocks and storehouses of intellectual capabilities, knowledge, experiences and energies that they brought to their work... [they are] also vessels that are conduits, flows and channels through which their intellectual capital [gets] communicated and emerge[s]."[57] The Indian entrepreneurs in the UAE played key roles as "vaults" and "vessels" to the UAE economy as well as the Indian economy.

India's foreign policy is now focusing more on the West Asian Gulf for new investment opportunities than on Europe. Girijesh Pant, Vice Chancellor of Doon University, stated in a Dubai conference that the Gulf is an economically beneficial area for India.[58] The global economy is shifting its focus from the West to the East. India has successfully placed itself as the next biggest economy to China. The GCC (Gulf Corporation Council) regions are also turning their attention towards India. As a result, today UAE is the second largest market for Indian products.[59] The UAE's growing demand for energy is another potential market for India. In the oil and gas sector, however, as India is one of the world's major hydrocarbon consumers, it needs to actively participate with the UAE.

An attempt is being made by the Indian entrepreneurs in the UAE together with their counterparts in India to form bilateral ties through two-way investments and joint ventures. An MOU has been signed between the Indian Chamber of Commerce and the IBPG (Indian Business Professional Group) in UAE, to provide support to Indian delegates visiting the UAE. It is important to note that the non-oil trade between India and UAE was worth over $ 26 billion in 2009.[60] Prominent companies from either country, like Punj Lloyd in India and Emaar and Nakheel in UAE, are successfully setting up their bases in each others' business sectors. The UAE is now pursuing business-friendly policies to initiate FDI and smoothen out the difficulties in setting up a business unit in the UAE that entrepreneurs face now. The application of economic and structural reform programmes, coupled with the increasingly effective role played by the private sector in materializing sustained development, have been instrumental in creating an attractive local and regional competitive investment environment.

Business Environment in the UAE

The overall impression of investors regarding the environment in the UAE is that it is "business-friendly". A majority of the interviewees have expressed their satisfaction with the business opportunities in UAE, except for a few objections such as limited citizenship rights and ownership restrictions. A brief overview of the business environment in the UAE has been presented below:

a) UAE has a stable economy characterized by a favourable business environment. The main driving forces there are a tax-free regime for investments in the UAE, no restriction on foreign currency transaction, and full repatriation of profit.
b) The business communities have a favourable perception of UAE from the standpoint of risks related to economy, finance, and investment.
c) The investment climate in the UAE is more favourable compared to other developing countries. The farsighted leaders of the UAE have pursued a market-oriented liberal policy and various diversified policies designed to attract foreign companies towards this region.
d) A favourable tax environment in the UAE especially in Free Trade Zones (FTZs) coupled with no corporate or income taxes further attracts global investors to the UAE.
e) Cost and acccss to finance is easy in the UAE. From a global standpoint, UAE has low disclosure standards towards protecting investors.
f) In UAE, timing and keeping workers are difficult. However, the position in UAE in this regard is better off compared to other GCC countries.
g) Some changes are necessary in processes of the court and legal system. The Dubai International Arbitration Centre (DIAC), however, follows the universal set rules laid down by the International Chamber of Commerce to solve business disputes quickly.
h) Based on the Executive Opinion Survey in the Arab world, the UAE has been placed first in the rankings for having the least burdensome administrative regulations and the lowest hidden import barrier. According to the Global Standards,

UAE ranks fourth for its least burdensome administrative regulations. Singapore, Hong Kong and Iceland being first, second and third in rank, respectively.

i) The UAE on the whole does not suffer from any problems regarding electricity and power supply. But recently, Sharjah has been facing some problems with its power supply.

j) The UAE has excellent transportation infrastructure which helps escalate business productivity in the UAE.

The above stated factors and ongoing reforms related to business investment have made the UAE an attractive business centre for investors.[61]

Conclusion

The focus of this chapter has been on the Indian entrepreneurs in the UAE who have proven themselves to be agents endowed with all the special capacities that entrepreneurs ought to possess to cope with the challenges, make the most of all available opportunities, and overcome the odds with calculated risks. A major section of these diasporic entrepreneurs in the UAE are engaged in service sectors. This may raise the question as to whether their activities should be considered innovative or not. To answer that, one must point to the fact that their unique business ideas prompted them to set forth in search of new market opportunities in an unknown land fraught with restrictions. Their dynamism in that respect is praiseworthy. They had to conceptualize newer ways to establish and conduct business in a new, largely unknown region where the culture and business atmosphere was totally different from that back in their homeland. Their cognitive skills guided them to identify the demands they could cater to in this land and seize the lucrative opportunities in appropriate time. Their honest intentions, values and ethics earned them a reputation for business as well as a unique position within this host society.

The Indian diasporic entrepreneurs' contribution towards the UAE economy has been immense. They have been engaged with the UAE economy since the pre-oil era, as money lenders and pearling industry investors and have supported the UAE people with their need for short term capital. They brought with them their knowledge, skills, and other associated capital as well as assumed a greater role in various developmental activities of this region. They not only provided much required commodities to urban areas but also stretched out their supplies to the more remote areas in the UAE.

This chapter must conclude with stress on the main points of this study: The Indian entrepreneurs in the UAE can act as a bridge between India and the UAE, however, their potential needs to be accentuated with better support from both their home and host countries. Pranab Mukherjee, Minister of External Affairs, India, stated in one of his lectures at the Emirates Centre for Strategic Studies and Research: "Two of the most important pre-requisites for continued high economic growth rate in India are energy security and development of infrastructure. India needs $500 billion in resources to meet the specific targets for infrastructural development and also needs to expand its electricity production. Here are the foundations of India's new terms of engagement with the Gulf region."[62] He iterated that the vast oil reserve of this region enabled the GCC countries, including the UAE, to generate excess funds, and that India wants to be in a long-term partnership with the UAE in the energy sector. He concluded the lecture by stating: "The challenge before us is to transform the present buyer-seller relationship into something more substantial and enduring, covering all economic sectors from energy to education and health."

This chapter re-establishes the fact that these entrepreneurs and business-class diaspora in the UAE can certainly play a key role in helping both countries to strengthen their relationship. They can act as a channel for flow of information, market intelligence, updates regarding changes/amendments in law, local rules and regulations, business environment and procedures between either country. India, in particular, could gain better results by aligning its interests with the potential of this diaspora in the UAE, engaging them with its developmental strategies.

ENDNOTES

1. Prakash C. Jain, ed., *Indian Diaspora in West Asia: A reader* (New Delhi: Manohar Publishers, 2007), 18.
2. Alan Alexander Milne, *Winnie-the-Pooh* (London: Methuen & Co., 1926).
3. John Kilby, as cited by Elizabeth Chell, Jean Haworth and Sally Brearley, in *The Entrepreneurial Personality: Concepts, Cases and Categories* (New York: Routledge, 1991), 2.
4. Richard Cantillon, as cited by Dwizendra Tripathi, in "An Integrated view of Entrepreneurship," *Economic and Political Weekly* 20, no. 48 (November 30, 1985): 163–68, www.jstor.org/stable437057 (accessed July 21, 2009).

5. Jean Baptiste, as cited by Tripathi, "Integrated view of Entrepreneurship," 163.
6. Marshall, as cited by Chell, Haworth and Brearley, *Entrepreneurial Personality*, 15–8.
7. *Ibid.*, 18.
8. Carl Meager, *Principles of Economics*, trans. J. Dingwall, B.F. Hoselitz and Glencoe (New York: Free Press, 1950), 8–14.
9. Joseph A Schumpeter, *The Theory of Economic Development* (Cambridge, MA: Harvard University Press, 1934), 66.
10. Chell, Haworth and Brearley, *Entrepreneurial Personality*, 19.
11. Joseph A. Schumpeter, "Crumbling Walls: The Obsolescence of the Entrepreneurial Function," in *Capitalism, Socialism and Democracy* (London: George Allen and Unwin [1943] 1976), 132.
12. Chell, Haworth and Brearley, *Entrepreneurial Personality*, 22.
13. *Ibid.*, 20.
14. Tripathi, "Integrated view of Entrepreneurship," 164.
15. Chell, Haworth and Brearley, *Entrepreneurial Personality*, 25.
16. *Ibid.*, 27.
17. P. Davidsson, M.B. Low and M. Wright, "Editors's Introduction: Low and MacMillan Ten Years on: Acheivements and Future Direction for Entrepreneurship Research," *Entrepreneurship Theory and Practice* 25, No. 4 (Summer 2001): 5–15.
18. Thomas Begley and David P. Boyd, as cited by James A.F. Stoner, R.E. Freeman and D.R. Gilbert Jr., *Management* (New Delhi: Prentice Hall of India Private Limited, 2001), 164.
19. *Ibid.*, 5.
20. Schumpeter, *Theory of Economic Development*, 66.
21. J.W. Carland, F. Hoy, W.R. Boulton and J.C. Carland, "Differentiating Entrepreneurs from Small Business Owners: A Conceptualization," *Academy of Management Review* 9, No. 2 (1984): 354–59.
22. Ram Buxani, *Taking the High Road* (Dubai: Motivate Publishing, 2003), 94–6.
23. *Ibid.*, 96.
24. *Ibid.*, 102.
25. *Ibid.*, 110.
26. Rosemarie Said Zahlan, *The Making of the Modern Gulf States* (London: Ithaca Press, 1998), 14.
27. "Abu Dhabi 2008–2009," Abu Dhabi Chamber of Commerce and Industry, and Information and Decision Support Center (2008), 3.
28. In an interview with Talmiz Ahmed, the Indian Ambassador to UAE, dated July 30, 2008.
29. *Gulf News*, "Emirates Stun Industry with $11.5b A380 Order: Deal for

32 More Super Jumbos makes Airline Biggest Buyer of Plane," June 09, 2010.

30. Source: UAE Year Book, 2008.
31. Source: Indian Embassy in the UAE.
32. "Abu Dhabi 2008–2009," 6.
33. International Monetary Fund, "United Arab Emirates: Selected Issues and Statistical Appendix," *IMF Country Report* No. 05/268 (August 2005): 5.
34. "Abu Dhabi: Business and Investment," Abu Dhabi Chamber of Commerce and Industry, and Information and Decision Support Center (2008), 22.
35. IMF, "United Arab Emirates: Selected Issues," 9.
36. "Abu Dhabi: Business and Investment," 23.
37. IMF, "United Arab Emirates: Selected Issues," 9.
38. "Abu Dhabi: Business and Investment," 20.
39. *Ibid.*, 21.
40. *Ibid.*, 21.
41. IMF, "United Arab Emirates: Selected Issues," 12.
42. "Abu Dhabi: Business and Investment," 9.
43. *Ibid.*, 9.
44. *Ibid.*, 10.
45. *Gulf News*, "New Law to limit UAE Public Debt: Company Law, Foreign Ownership," June 18, 2010.
46. "Abu Dhabi: Business and Investment," 10.
47. *Ibid.*, 10.
48. Michael Smith and Alexis Waller, "Recent Development in UAE Property Law", *Economic Focus*, Arab-British Chamber of Commerce Publications (September 2007), published online by *Clyde and Co*, http://www.clydeco.com/knowledge/articles/recent dcvelopments-in-uae-property-law.cfm (accessed February 15, 2009).
49. *Ibid.*, 1.
50. *Ibid.*, 5.
51. "Abu Dhabi: Business and Investment," 13.
52. *Ibid.*, 16.
53. *Ibid.*, 18.
54. "UAE Business Forecast Report: Q1 2009," Business Monitor International (October, 2008).
55. Buxani, *Taking the High Road*, 99–100.
56. P.P. McDougall and B.M. Oviatt, "International Entrepreneurship: The Intersection of Two Research Paths," *Academy of Mangement Journal* 43, no. 5 (2000): 902–06.
57. Maria Aggestam and James J. Keenan, "Entrepreneurial Mindsets During Environmental Jolts: Vessels and Vaults," in *New Movements in*

Entrepreneurship, eds. Chris Steyaert and Daniel Hjorth (Cheltenham, Glos: Edward Elgar, 2003), 260.

58. *Gulf News*, "India set to Target East Asia and Gulf for New Investment," June 18, 2009.
59. Interview with Talmiz Ahmed.
60. Source: Indian Business and Professional Group (IBPG)
61. IMF, "United Arab Emirates: Selected Issues," *IMF Country Report* No. 05/268: 10–2.
62. Pranab Mukherjee, in a speech at Emirates Centre for Strategic Studies and Research (ECSSR), Abu Dhabi, May 26, 2008.

6

Fieldwork Analysis and Findings

The findings of this analysis are based on the survey conducted in the three major emirates of the United Arab Emirates: namely Abu Dhabi, Dubai and Sharjah. The survey was primarily conducted through a series of interviews with the Indian entrepreneurs based in the UAE, some of whom moved to this region during the pre-oil era, and others who migrated in the post-oil era. The views of the "newer generation" entrepreneurs—mostly the children of established entrepreneurs in the UAE—have also been taken into consideration while interviewing their parents.

1. Profile of Indian Entrepreneurs in the UAE

Table 6.1: Educational qualifications

High School Diploma	4	16%
Undergraduate Degree	13	52%
Graduate/Postgraduate Degree	8	32%
Total Number of Representatives	**25**	**100%**

As shown in the above Table 6.1, 52 per cent of the respondents hold an undergraduate degree, 32 per cent hold a graduate/post graduate degree (the majority of whom are young entrepreneurs who are the children of established businessmen in the UAE), and the remaining 16 per cent of respondents are high school diploma holders. It was observed that a majority of them did not have a particularly high level of educational qualification. As it appears, formal education had a minimal influence on them as the sector of business they engaged in did not particularly require higher education so long they adequately possessed the knowledge and skills required to conduct their business. Also, since they had relatively lesser avenues open to technically oriented careers they opted for entrepreneurial careers. The third factor is that most of them came from business backgrounds and had informal entrepreneurial education.

In spite of the minimum role played by formal education noticed in our study, it has to be acknowledged that education helps in sharpening and broadening the knowledge level of the entrepreneurs. This supports my earlier point about the shift in the importance of education over time and although some individuals may be "born to be entrepreneurs", some entrepreneurs can be created through education which will facilitate in bringing more entrepreneurial talents into the economy.

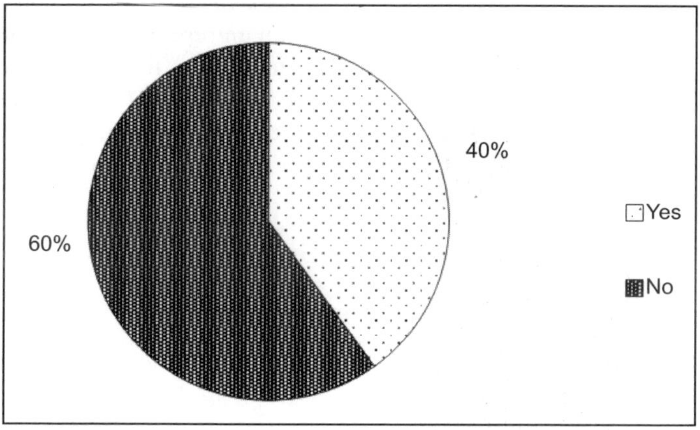

Chart 6.1: Previous experience under another entrepreneur

Charts 6.1, 6.2 and 6.3, show that Indian entrepreneurs in the UAE lack formal entrepreneurial training and pre-entrepreneurial travel experience. On the basis of the above findings, it can be inferred that they have remarkable inherent characteristics of entrepreneurs although they did not have skill based competencies due to a lack of proper formal training and travel experiences. Instead, their socio-cultural background gave them informal training. Most of them came from business backgrounds and their association with business environments might have provided the required informal training to run their businesses. They had immense learning competencies which are in-born attributes of an entrepreneur and honed competencies

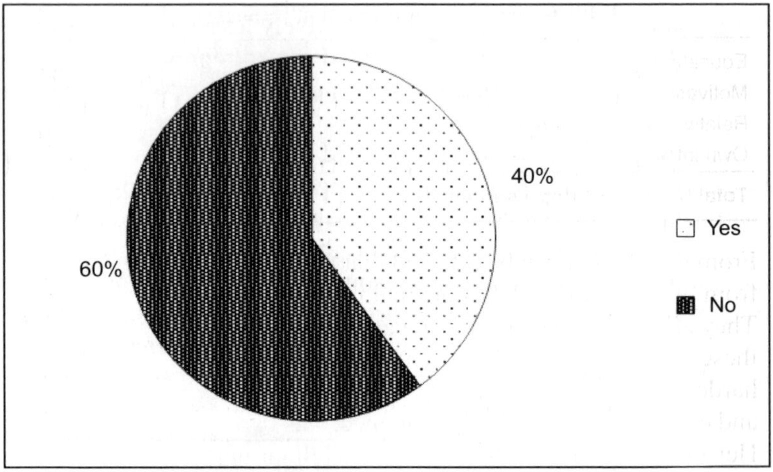

Chart 6.2: Underwent training in previous jobs

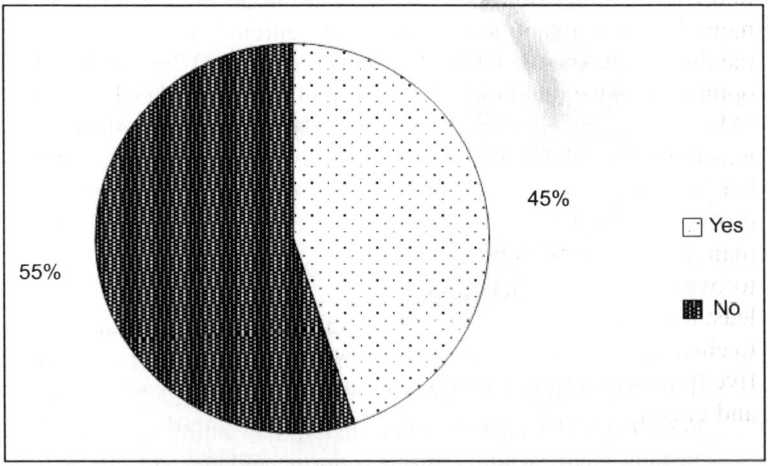

Chart 6.3: Spent time outside India before coming to the UAE

through their experiences. Seeing their success in the UAE, we can draw the conclusion that the entrepreneurs are born and entrepreneurial competencies are sharpened through travel and training.

Table 6.2 highlights that the larger section of the Indian Entrepreneurs of the UAE embarked on their business venture due to their own interest (48%), followed by inspiration from successful fellow entrepreneurs (20%), education (16%) and relatives (16%).

Table 6.2: Sources of inspiration for their business

Education	4	16%
Motivation from success of fellow entrepreneurs	5	20%
Relatives	4	16%
Own interest	12	48%
Total Number of Representatives	**25**	**100%**

From this data, it can be inferred that their interest for business came from 'inner urges' and they are mainly guided by "need achievement". They are distinctive in several ways. They liked to shoulder risks and these risks encouraged and stimulated them for greater effort and harder work. It has to be acknowledged that the role of the family, and especially the mother's influence, was paramount in this respect. Her influence in their becoming self-reliant nurtured their desire to become entrepreneurs. Thus, it is not only the inner urges but also family and socio-cultural factors that conditioned their entrepreneurial mentality. The example of famous entrepreneurs like B.R. Shetty, the director of the New Medical Centre group in Abu Dhabi and the opinion of others supports the argument. According to B.R. Shetty, "My mother played a key role in my entrepreneurial career .When I was facing problems arranging for funds, my mother wanted to sell her jewellery and valuable properties to support me in my time of crisis. But I did not accept her financial support, I thought I am a man, it is my responsibility to support myself. I personally managed to overcome such crisis .She used to tell me to provide food to at least ten families around me. She commented it is beyond my control to change the whole world. Today I am supporting more than twenty five thousand families, today I am here due to my mother's support and encouragement."

Table 6.3: Reactions of social group to the entrepreneur's job

Encouragement	19	76%
Objection	4	16%
Indifference	2	8%
Total Number of Representatives	**25**	**100%**

Based on Table 6.3 it is to be noted that a major section of Indian entrepreneurs (76%) of the UAE received significant encouragement from social surroundings, the next section of the respondents (16%)

received objections from social surroundings and the rest (8%) felt indifference from those around them. The above responses suggest that those in the majority section had entrepreneurial backgrounds. Their socio-cultural settings were in favour of the emergence of entrepreneurs and this gave them the support to become entrepreneurs. The 16 per cent of respondents who received objection from social surroundings either belonged to non business backgrounds or members of their society might have come across some entrepreneurs who were unsuccessful in their life .Their previous learning experience and fear of insecurity developed negative perceptions about this career.

Table 6.4: Reasons to choose to be an entrepreneur

Personal inclination	25	100%
Persuasion from relatives	0	0%
Following family business	0	0%
Total Number of Representatives	**25**	**100%**

Table 6.4 represents that personal inclination was the overwhelming reason which attracted the respondents towards the field of entrepreneurship. 100 per cent of the interviewees did not cite any factor other than own inclination to choose the career of an entrepreneur in the survey. However, during my discussions with them, they acknowledged that a profit motive as a well as the desire to gain status and prestige in the society might have influenced them.

2. Nature of the Business

Table 6.5: Business Sector

Trade	14	56%
Industry	6	24%
Finance	2	8%
Health	1	4%
Travel	2	8%
Total Number of Representatives	**25**	**100%**

Table 6.5 represents the contribution of the Indian entrepreneurs in the UAE towards the Indian and UAE economy. The major sectors where Indian Entrepreneurs are engaged in are trade (56%), followed by industry (24%). Finance and Travel sectors represent the same per cent of the respondents' fields (8%). The health sector represents the

least preferred area of investment for the respondents. Based on the above statistics, the researcher hypothesized on the many factors influence these entrepreneurs to prefer the trade sector for investment. The classic Indian entrepreneurs came into the Gulf area as traders. As mentioned in an earlier chapter, Indian merchant groups enjoyed immense prestige and status in the UAE society. These aspects might have motivated post-oil entrepreneurs to prefer this sector. The previous experience of traditional entrepreneurs about UAE's market opportunity might have guided and inspired other entrepreneurs to invest in the trade sector. Another factor is that the trade sector does not require heavy investment. It can be concluded that the expectation of larger profit, easy management of the business and prestige level in their society would have motivated them to be attracted to this sector. Furthermore, classical entrepreneurs had already established themselves as successful entrepreneurs. Thus, their success encouraged other entrepreneurs to engage in the trading sector.

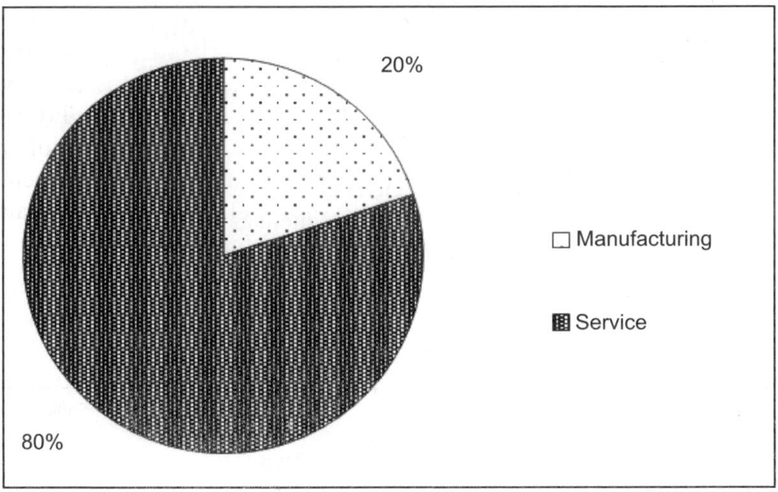

Chart 6.4: Main output

The pie chart 6.4 shows that the service sector occupies 80 per cent as compared to the manufacturing sector which occupies 20 per cent as the response distribution for the primary sector that the entrepreneurs are involved in. On the basis of the above data, it can be stated that the non-availability of permanent status (citizenship rights) might have discouraged them from long term investment in the UAE market, namely in the manufacturing sector which typically requires more fixed investments with long payback periods. Furthermore, the manufacturing sector requires heavy upfront investment and many other factors such as low availability of technically skilled staff in the local market discouraged them from investing in the manufacturing sector. Due to the lack of sufficient funds available to them, they opted to invest in the service sector where the required infrastructure already exists. Thus, the major primary sector where many Indian entrepreneurs are engaged in is the service sector.

Table 6.6: Types of ownership

Sole trader	6	24%
Partnership	14	56%
Corporation	5	20%
Total Number of Representatives	**25**	**100%**

Table 6.6 represents the fact that the forms of business ownership run by Indian entrepreneurs in the UAE consist of partnerships (56%), followed by sole trading (24%). Only 20 per cent of Indian entrepreneurs run their business as a corporation. The researcher believes that the scope of innovation is limited in sole trade. So the new generation of entrepreneurs who are mostly the children of the established entrepreneurs of the UAE are trying to move away from the traditional path of running an establishment as a sole trader. During the interviews, some of them said that they wanted independence and wanted to start a new partnership business with their fellow group members. The desire to introduce new approaches to business guided them to opt for a partnership. Another factor played a key role in this process; the chance of expansion with limited risk factor has motivated them to follow a middle path.

Table 6.7: Sources of capital

Owners' funds	17	68%
Borrowed funds – relatives	4	16%
Borrowed funds – other individuals	3	12%
Borrowed funds – institutions	1	4%
Total Number of Representatives	**25**	**100%**

In response to the question asked about their resources of finance 68 per cent of respondents remark that they relied heavily on their own funds, 16 per cent borrowed from relatives and 12 per cent borrowed either from non-relatives or from their own community people. Only 4 per cent were dependent on institutional loans to set up their businesses. Based on the above table, it can be stated that the Indian entrepreneur's class in the UAE are financially resourceful. During our discussions, they mentioned that most of them use "family resources" initially. Many of them came from merchant families who have long business histories in India or other parts of the world.

Table 6.8: Innovation techniques introduced

Marketing	14	56%
Management	4	16%
Research and development	2	8%
Collection of Raw Materials	2	8%
Channels of Distribution	0	0%
Diversification	3	12%
Total Number of Representatives	**25**	**100%**

Another important question whose answers were sought from them asked about the innovation technique that they introduced into their establishment. Many respondents gave multiple answers to this question. As shown in the data collected, 56 per cent employed innovation in marketing, 16 per cent in management, 12 per cent diversified, 8 per cent concentrated on R&D, and 8 per cent on the collection of raw materials. Channels of distribution were the least preferred area (0%) for introduction of innovative techniques. The fact that multiple answers were provided by the entrepreneurs reveals that they introduced innovative technique in multiple segments of their business. They believed that their innovation efforts should encompass the business as a whole. They noted that they focused their attention on innovation in the marketing segment only to achieve a competitive edge over others in the UAE market. They also stated that the aggressive marketing strategies that they used concentrated on delivering quality products and in the creation of "customer delight".

Table 6.9: Capital intensity in the entrepreneur's firm.

Heavy investment and long term scale of return	9	36%
Little investment with high capital turnover rate	12	48%
Investment for nominal return	4	16%
Total Number of Representatives	**25**	**100%**

Table 6.9 shows that 48 per cent of respondents are in favour of minimum investment with high turnover rate, as compared to heavy investment over the long term (36%). A minority section of respondents (16%) preferred investment for nominal return. The researcher believes that though the UAE business environment is favourable for investment, the local partnership system (except Free Zones) and non-permanent status of NRIs discourages them from investing on a long term basis. Other factors are that although the UAE has political stability, the political condition of the neighbouring countries of the UAE reduces the confidence level of the investors when investing on a long-term basis. Moreover, the entrepreneurs are primarily engaged in the trade sector. Their attitudes are shaped by the characteristics of this sector which is quick maximum return within the minimum time. As a result, they are not in a mental position to go for heavy long-term investment.

The chart 6.5 represents that the entrepreneurs relied heavily on intuition (55%) rather than calculation (45%) when making decisions. They commented that initially, calculation plays an important role in

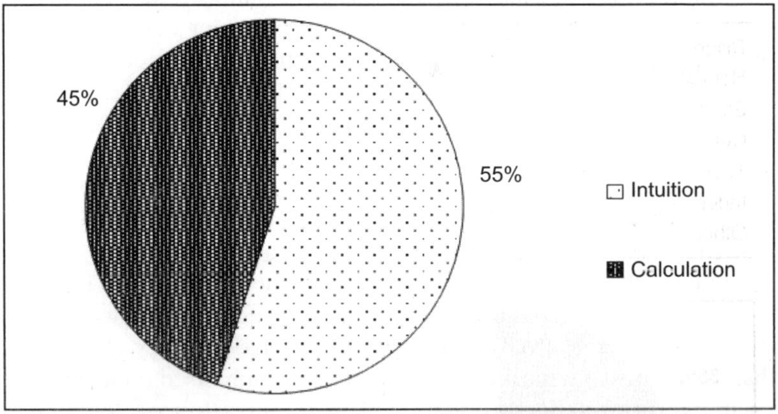

Chart 6.5: Primary influence on decision making process

making any investment decision but ultimately, intuition dominates the decision making process. These above remarks further support my previous point that entrepreneurial qualities are inborn and can be refined through training.

Table 6.10 shows that 44 per cent of the interviewees favoured employing their own funds to expand their business. 24 per cent want to depend on borrowed funds followed by funds from shareholders

Table 6.10: Sources of capital if entrepreneur chooses to expand their business.

Shareholders	5	20%
New Partners	3	12%
Own Funds	11	44%
Borrowed Funds	6	24%
Total Number of Representatives	**25**	**100%**

at 20 per cent and new partners at 12 per cent. The above table re-establishes the fact that Indian entrepreneurs of the UAE have enough financial strength to operate their own business outside India. Another important factor that was noticed was that they showed high confidence about their business which might have come from their confidence in their own financial strengths.

As shown in the data collected, honesty and sincerity are the two most valued characteristics that the entrepreneurs seek in their business associates.

Table 6.11: Characteristics sought after in business associates.[1]

Diligence	9
Honesty	18
Sincerity	13
Communication Skills	11
Technical Capacity	9
Independence	3
Others	3

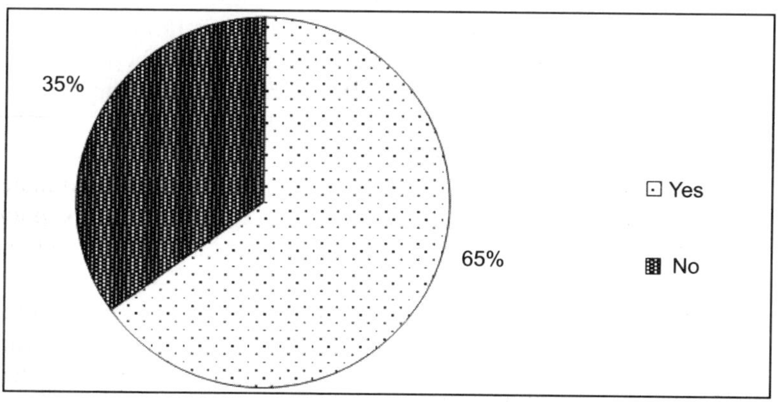

Chart 6.6: Encountered problems finding technically skilled staff in the UAE

From the Table 6.11 it can be noted that 65 per cent of the respondents faced difficulties in arranging for technically skilled staff in the local market whereas 35 per cent of them said that they did not face such difficulty. The section of entrepreneurs who didn't face many difficulties was probably engaged in business where requirements for technical staff are minimal.

3. Perceptions about India

Table 6.12 represents the major contributions of Indian entrepreneurs of the UAE. Of the total respondents, 40 per cent created job opportunities for Indian workers, 32 per cent invested in the Indian economy (either in real estate or in joint businesses) and 28 per cent commented that their contributions can be seen in various field. These entrepreneurs facilitated and helped to increase flow of Indian goods in the UAE market and thus by providing quality goods they acted as a mediator to build the image of India in the UAE market. On the basis of the above table, the contribution to India can be summarised as follows:

Firstly, they increased trade and investment in their home country.

Secondly, they contributed to the balance of payment through fund transfer and supported remaining family members and relatives in their home country.

Thirdly, they provided various opportunities to the Indians in the UAE market and thus contributed in the human resource development and played an important role in the labour market of their home country.

Fourthly, they provided information about business opportunities of the UAE to the future investors of India and thus played an important role in reducing the opportunistic behaviour for the agents of India. Thus, by transmitting valuable information to the people (especially to their own region), they created opportunities for them for profitable international trade.

Finally, they created investment opportunities for nostalgic trade. Nostalgic trade refers to the export of the home country. The success

Table 6.12: Entrepreneur's primary contribution to India

Job Creation	10	40%
Investment	8	32%
Other (e.g. image creation, export increase, infrastructure, etc...)	7	28%
Total Number of Representatives	**25**	**100%**

of few entrepreneurs motivated other entrepreneurs to invest in home country and thus created export business for India. Thus Indian entrepreneurs staying as NRI, constantly struggle to make their own fortune and work harder for the creation of goodwill of India.

The above mentioned points reflect the positive contribution of Indian entrepreneurs of the UAE towards Indian economy.

On the basis of the Chart 6.7, it is noted that 56 per cent commented that they are not treated at par with the diasporic entrepreneurs of advanced countries, while 24 per cent were indifferent about this question and 20 per cent commented that they

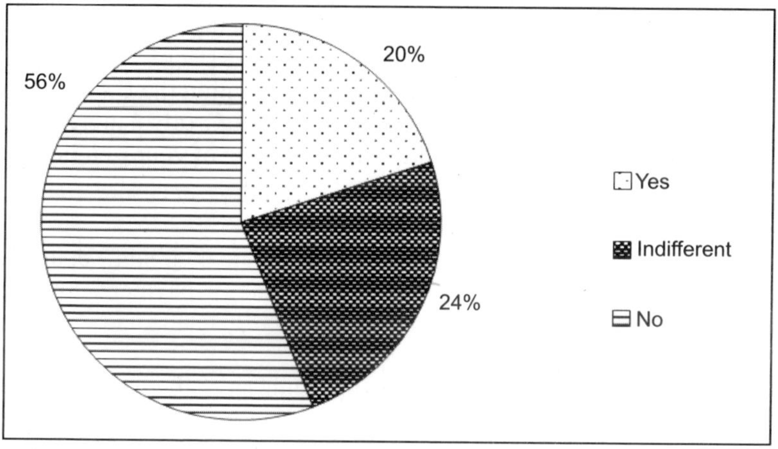

Chart 6.7: People who feel recognized as valuable contributors to India by the Indian Government (as compared to UK/US based Indians).

didn't face any such discrimination. A few select anonymous quotes from my interviewees are as follows:[2]

"Gulf entrepreneurs have been treated as 'second class citizens' whereas entrepreneurs from the UK and USA enjoy the superior citizen status in India."

"We are merely treated as India's step-sons in India."

"I have never come across any initiatives or directives from the Indian government to advise and/or protect Indian entrepreneurs in the UAE."

"Obviously we Gulf based NRIs contribute more to India's Forex than UK or USA based NRIs but when it comes to recognition and meeting our requirements or solving them, we have always been ignored due to Indian bureaucracy. We have to satisfy the ego and power needs of junior officials of the bureaucratic department which demotivates our interest on investment in India".

As is evident from these quotes, the Indian government has not taken any step to support these entrepreneurs and is thus losing the opportunity to capitalize on the valuable resources that are the Indian entrepreneurs of the UAE.

4. Perceptions about the UAE

The Entrepreneur's Primary Contributions to the UAE

The primary contributions cited by the entrepreneurs that were interviewed for this study were "money provided to local partners" (as local partners are required to own at least 51% of businesses), "the provision of a variety of quality products within the UAE", "the improvement of bilateral relations with India" (also increasing awareness of the UAE within India) and "training of young engineers of the UAE".

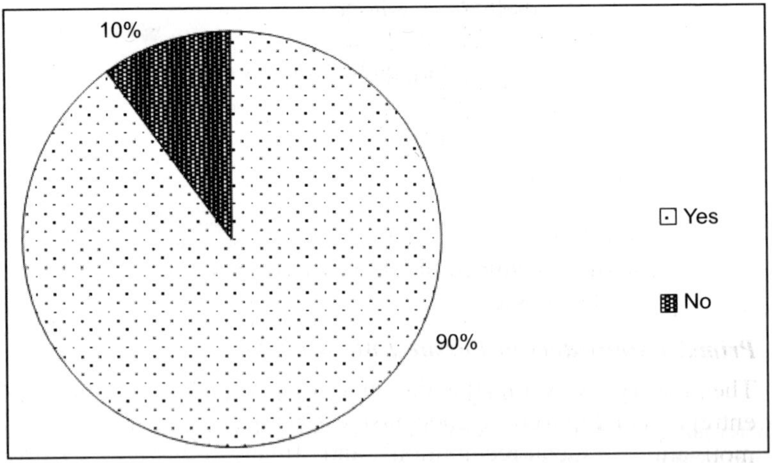

Chart 6.8: Does the Entrepreneur think that the UAE economic environment is supportive to the growth of entrepreneurs?

In response to the question about whether or not the economic environment of the UAE is favourable for investment, 90 per cent of the respondents commented that it is indeed business friendly and supportive to the growth of entrepreneurship. The remaining 10 per cent of respondents expressed their dissatisfaction about UAE's economic environment. Considering the view of the majority of respondents, it is apparent that UAE nurtures entrepreneurial culture and supports and encourages entrepreneurs. Other than a few negative factors such as citizenship rights, property rights, and the sponsorship system, their attitude towards the economic environment of the UAE is favourable.

Table 6.13: Nationalities primarily comprising workforce

Indian	24	96%
Other	1	4%
Total Number of Representatives	**25**	**100%**

From the above table it is noted that most of the Indian entrepreneurs tend to favour Indian workers in their businesses. The largest segment of the respondents (96%) primarily employed Indian workers in their businesses followed by (4%) of the respondent who primarily employed workers from other nationalities. During the interview sessions, the researcher got extra information regarding the preference towards Indian workers. Select opinions are represented below:

a) Due to the similar cultural background, they preferred Indian workers in their businesses. The workers can easily fit within a similar business culture and environment.
b) Indian workers are docile by nature and easy to manage.
c) The wages of workers of other nationalities are generally higher compared to Indian workers.
d) Finally, patriotism was an important element in this process. Every entrepreneur wanted to provide some services to their homeland. The non-pecuniary motive to help their community guided them to employ more Indian workers in their businesses.

Primary Motivators to Pursue Entrepreneurship

The primary motivators that the interviewees mentioned in pursuing entrepreneurship were "a good business environment", "achievement motivation", "social recognition", and "financial gain".

Table 6.14: Reasons for moving to the UAE

Greener Pastures	20	80%
More Opportunities	2	8%
Better Business Environment	2	8%
Security	1	4%
Total Number of Representatives	**25**	**100%**

The above table shows that 80 per cent of the respondents came to the UAE in search of greener pastures, 8 per cent of the interviewees came to this region in search of more opportunities prevalent in the UAE market, 8 per cent favoured UAE for better business environment and 4 per cent came for security reasons. It can be inferred that the UAE's economic environment was favourable to Indian entrepreneurs and it shows that the UAE government successfully created a good image of it. Though India is emerging as one of the "Asian Giants", the discrepancy of the income levels in India and UAE can be cited as an another factor for Indians to move out from India and come to the UAE. They took a venture to come and invest in the UAE with the hope that the potential for earning more income in the UAE was much higher than that in India.

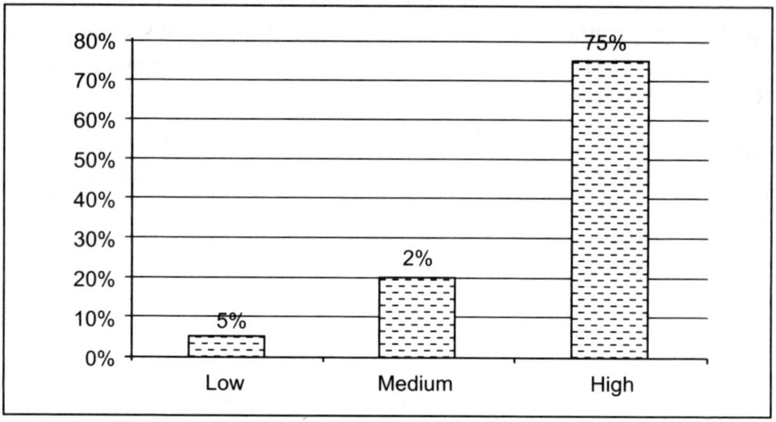

Chart 6.9: Business prospects in the UAE

The above chart represents that 75 per cent of respondents believe that business prospects in the UAE is bright, while 20 per cent of the respondents believe that the UAE economy has medium prospects for investment and the remaining 5 per cent of respondents commented that the UAE economy has low business prospects. Based on the above chart, it can be assessed that overall impressions of the Indian firms about UAE's economic environment are satisfactory but regarding a few aspects, the entrepreneurs hold a common view that the most important resistance factor to investing in the UAE's economy is the ownership restriction on non-nationals. Considering the weight of the favourable factors, it can be represented that UAE is nonetheless business-friendly.

Challenges Faced for Working in the UAE

a) Citizenship rights: Citizenship is not provided to non-locals which reduces business confidence as permanent visas are never guaranteed.
b) High rent and accommodation costs: As ownership of land was previously not allowed in places other than the Free Zone, this challenge was one of the primary obstacles the entrepreneurs faced.
c) Language: Lack of working knowledge of the Arabic language causes communication barriers.
d) Lack of skilled personnel in the local market: The entrepreneurs have to sponsor employees who are brought in from abroad which is expensive.

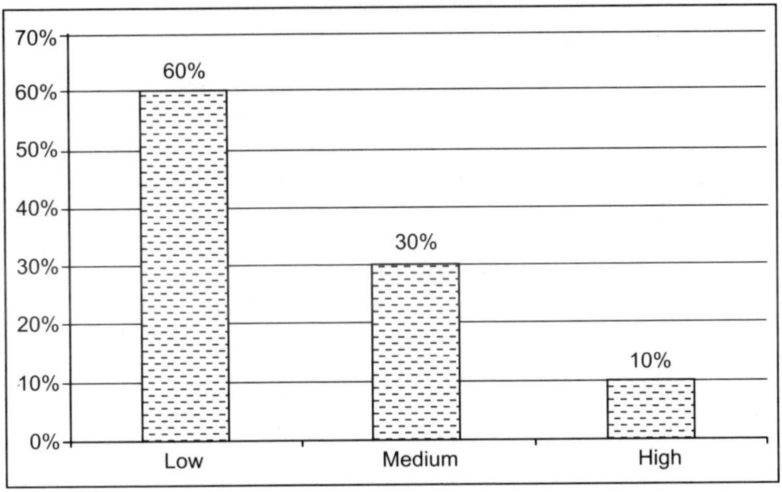

Chart 6.10: Difficulty dealing with the legal challenges

It is noted from the above chart that 60 per cent of the respondents feel that there are minimal difficulties when dealing with legal challenges in the UAE. The minority (10%) do not think that the legal challenges are easy to deal with. The intermediate group (30%) expressed their opinion in between. Based on the above references, it can be concluded that although the UAE needs some transparency in legal affairs, Indian entrepreneurs are comfortable running their businesses there.

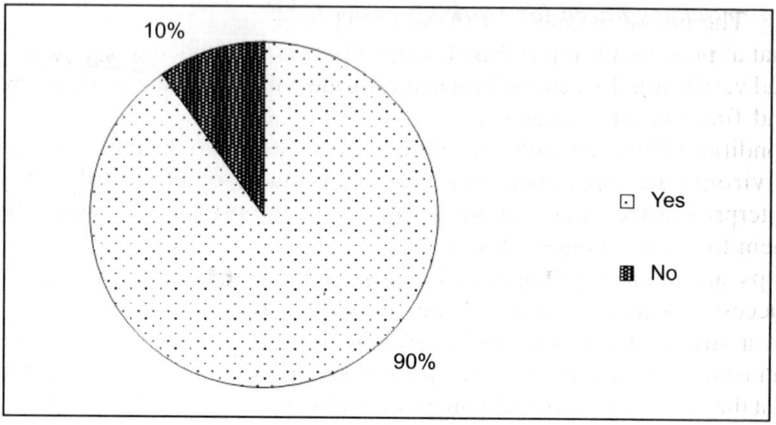

Chart 6.11: Is there scope for innovation in the UAE?

In response to the question regarding the scope of innovation in the UAE, 90 per cent of the respondents answered that it has a large scope for innovation. Only 10 per cent of the respondents gave negative answers. From the above findings, it can be inferred that most of the Indian entrepreneurs probably belong to trade and service sectors which do not require remarkable innovation. The activities of this sector and some service sectors depend on traditional modes of operation. That is why the majority of Indian entrepreneurs did not face much difficulty in introducing moderate innovation for their business and believe scope for innovation in the UAE is high.

Conclusion

From the above survey as a whole, the following general observations about the Indian entrepreneurs of the UAE can be made.

The Indian entrepreneurial class of the UAE can be considered as an asset to both India and the UAE. This highly energetic group uprooted themselves from their country of origin and ventured to set their feet in an unknown world .Till now, the majority of Indians are not familiar with all the emirates of the UAE, apart from Dubai. The Indian entrepreneurs of the UAE had higher strategic vision which guided them to take advantage of the opportunities prevalent in the UAE market .Their unique capabilities turned them into one of the richest business communities in the Gulf region though the journey towards this path was not an easy one. Numerous obstacles stood in their way.

The market scenario of the old UAE was totally different from that at present. Entrepreneurs had to operate in a system where they had very limited access to information regarding technology, markets and finance, and suffered enormous emotional stress due to such conditions. Despite these hurdles, they successfully analysed the environment and could correctly set the action plans of their enterprises. They had the opportunity to seek potential, which led them to see the market prospects of the UAE, correctly identify the gaps and supply the needed requirements to customers. They successfully leveraged a competitive advantage and derived benefits on a sustainable basis. They did not employ overtly aggressive innovative techniques in their businesses but it has to be acknowledged that they did show innovation in the creation of new products, markets, services and techniques in management.

Other than these factors, two important assets were prevalent among the Indian business community. The most important aspects required to operate in the global economy are "global mindsets" and "trust in one's business partner". These two attributes are highly prevalent among the Indian entrepreneurs of the UAE. From the pre-oil era they successfully created trust-based relationships which placed them in unique positions in society. The relationship between the ruler and the merchant community can be better understood with the comment made by Yusuf Ali M.A., managing director of EMKE group. He said, "I have always maintained very cordial relationships with all the rulers and members of the ruling family and they have always given me a patient hearing whenever I have gone to them for any issue concerning us expats, be it for allocating land for Hindu cremation ground or for building churches, for community centres or for any other welfare measures. Many countries in the world could take lessons from the way our rulers here have led this great country." The business community in Dubai and the royal family there in particular have a special bond (described in the previous chapter). Indian entrepreneurs could successfully adapt themselves to living in UAE society. The previous experience of living in India among various regional diversities helped them to stay together peacefully with other nationalities while keeping their individual identity. Each individual is unique in the sense that each individual used his/her unique capability to create something new. They successfully took calculated risks for their businesses, worked harder and coordinated and directed transaction between their business and the market. They accepted working longer hours, knowing very well that their future is uncertain, and successfully balanced positive and negative consequences.

Entrepreneurial work is not fit for everyone. It is to be acknowledged that Indian values and the culture have played an important role in shaping and moulding the entrepreneurs' thinking and behaviour. They are dynamic, have persistence and perseverance, and are thrifty, forward looking, aware of mutual responsibilities, duties and obligations, and have a sense of shame if they fail to fulfil obligations. All these factors have contributed towards the Indian entrepreneurs' successes in the UAE. They successfully built trust for themselves that gave them a unique status in the UAE society and acted as brand ambassadors for India.

On the basis of the field survey, it can be summarised that these entrepreneurs are highly resourceful and believe in their own emotional and intellectual capabilities. They had high strategic vision which led them to set their goal correctly. They are an asset to India, and can act as key players in the developmental process of India if India can successfully harness their resources. Such strategic assets can deliver maximum benefits to India only through setting up the proper institutional support mechanism and when appropriate policies are formulated by the government of India. The book expects these empirical findings to have theoretical and practical implications for future researchers who have an interest in the entrepreneurial strength of Indians, the Indian policy makers, local and international non-profit organisation and various financial institutions. Future studies should further enlighten this conceptual framework.

ENDNOTES

1. Each of the interviewees gave multiple answers to this survey question, hence percentages could not be derived.
2. Names of the interviewees have been withheld upon request.

7

Policy Recommendation

At present, there is a lot of literature available on diaspora and entrepreneurship.[1] Studies regarding diasporic entrepreneurs have grown tremendously in quantity over the last few years; with many highlighting the significant gaps in our understanding of the diasporic entrepreneurs in the UAE. Furthermore, no similar study could be traced among the available literature on UAE, although some migration studies on the Gulf have been conducted.[2] Literature available on the Indian diaspora largely concentrates on Indians in the UK, USA, Canada, etc., but has paid scant attention to the incipient Indian diaspora in the UAE. This study has been attempting to shed some light on the otherwise unexplored realities of the Indian diaspora in the UAE. As discussed earlier in this study, the Indian government is not well positioned to capitalize fully on the Indian entrepreneurs in the UAE. Hence an attempt has been made here to create awareness of the roles that the Indian entrepreneurs in the UAE could play and suggestions have been made regarding what measures the Indian government can take to fully utilize them.

Before discussing policy recommendations, it is necessary to have a clear view of the various resources possessed by this diaspora. Though the main focus of this study has been the economic contribution made by these diasporic entrepreneurs, in order to better understand this aspect the study also discusses in brief their associated resources and contributions. There is a consensus of opinion that the individual and collective resources of the diaspora can contribute a lot in various fields such as economic growth, poverty reduction, social development, human empowerment, and socio-economic equality. According to Orozco, "The economic contribution of diaspora can be summarized under the 'Five T's', 'Tourism, Transportation, Telecommunication, Trade and Transmission of money remittance."[3]

Diasporic Entrepreneurial Capital

A) Human Capital

Human capital refers to the productive attributes of a person from the point of view of the economy. According to Dina Ionescu, "Interest in human capital should involve movements of both skilled and unskilled migrants, notwithstanding the current policy bias on highly qualified migrants, whose number have greatly increased and given rise to what is generally referred to as Brain Drain."[4] The contribution made by the educated diaspora are seldom appreciated, instead, they are listed under the category of "brain drain" and criticized as negative to economic development. Critics argue that the significant resources spent towards their education cannot be compensated alone by what they contribute to their homeland.[5] Nowadays the "brain drain" concept is being replaced by a new concept—"brain circulation". The IT sector in Bangalore, India, has been credited for their contribution towards developing a networking linkage with the Indian workers in Silicon Valley. Such activities create positivity in the minds of the policy makers in developing countries towards their expatriate communities, thereafter the diasporas are regarded as assets. There is no solid evidence, however, that this highly educated group of individuals, who are considered to constitute a brain drain, do indeed mobilize their resources towards their home country on a regular basis. According to Deepak Nayyar, "There is little that is addressed to the low-skill, low-income, temporary migrant, mostly workers in the Middle East who provide the substantial amount of foreign exchange in the form of unrequired transfer and reenter the labour market in search of employment on their return. The asymmetry is worth noting."[6] The focus on the highly educated class while assessing diaspora impedes the assessment of the potentials of the other sections of diaspora who belong to the unskilled and semi-skilled group. The contributions of these unskilled workers are immense. World Wide Remittance data supports the arguments. In the context of UAE, it can be stated that their contribution towards their homeland can be increased if their potentials are assessed properly by the home country.

B) Financial and Entrepreneurial Capital of the Diaspora

The financial contribution by the diaspora include Foreign Direct Investment (FDI), creation of trade and investment, remittances, savings, investment in real estate and various kinds of charitable activities. Remittances made by migrant workers have received much attention from the international communities. Information on the contributions of the diaspora in the UAE is limited; however the global trend shows that the contributions, in terms of FDIs and remittances, made by diasporic entrepreneurs have increased over the years. FDIs have been increasing at the global level, for example from $106 billion in 1995 to $143 billion in 2002. However, compared to the FDIs, the global flow of remittances observed over the same period of time show a higher increment, from $48 billion to $80 billion.[7] Many scholars have argued that the Indian contribution in terms of FDIs has been far less compared to that in China. "In 2002, about half of the $48 billion FDI in China was contributed by the Chinese diasporas, but in comparison, only 10 percent of India's $4.43 billion FDI in 2002 was generated by the Indian diasporas."[8] It must be stated that the Chinese diasporas mainly comprise business groups, whereas the Indian diasporas are largely professionals, causing the disparity in comparison. Investments made by the diasporas is an economic decision dependent on factors such as self interest, profit or altruistic motives that lead them to invest in either business ventures or social projects. This study would like to argue that if the right incentives are provided by the Indian government to the Indian diasporas to motivate their decision to invest, the flow of FDIs into India too will rise.

C) Social Capital

Social capital refers to the "network together with shared norms, value and understanding that facilitate cooperation within and among groups."[9] Trust and shared confidence is the basis for the development of social capital. According to Zachariah, Mathew and Rajan, "network connection can be considered as a form of social capital which people can draw upon to gain information as well as material or psychological support".[10] This concept of social capital is very important in the context of contribution by the diasporas towards their home and host countries. The social capital among the diaspora enables the individuals to retain contact with their hometown and interact with their host society. Mutual trust and social ties enhance investment and foreign trade, and play a key role in reducing transaction costs. In the words of Dina Ionescu, "two main types of social capital influence what may be referred to as either bonding or bridging in relation to diaspora: families and friends—bonding; and communities and institutions in the host country—bridging. These may be mutually supportive or may work against each other and influence individual attitude towards home and host communities."[11]

D) Affective Capital

Every diaspora possesses affective capital which is reflected in their interest in their home country, a sense of responsibility for bringing about betterment in their motherland. This feeling may be triggered by various emotional factors among those staying away from their homelands. Affective capital can be utilized productively towards both the host region and home country and an overall sense of goodwill can be created. The High Level Committee on Indian Diaspora was set up in 2001 with the intention of exploring ways to negotiate with them in the best possible way. This committee noticed that there were "deep and binding ties with a commitment to India's welfare and a reserve of goodwill amongst the Indian diaspora deeply entrenched and waiting to be tapped."[12]

Their sentimental link with their home country is strong enough to create a nostalgic market in the host country. The demand for various home-country products could facilitate investment in the home country either by the diaspora/diasporic entrepreneurs or by the homegrown manufacturers. This in turn would generate employment opportunities in the home as well as the host countries and could become another source of revenue generation.

A good trade relation between the two countries can bring about desired results. For example, at the Dubai Shopping Festival, the Indian Pavilion attracts many customers of different nationalities and acts as a network builder in this process. However, to further succeed in this area, productive capacity and quality control maintaining the standard of the product need to be strengthened.

E) Local Capital

According to Dina Ionescu, "The notion of local capital attracts attention to the fact that diasporas are often inclined to make investment at the local level, usually in a region or locality of origin, where they still have family ties and are familiar with the local context." The studies conducted by various organizations—the survey of Lusophone Diaspora Networks and Associations undertaken in 2006 by IOM, Lisbon; the MIDA Italy Program targeting African diasporas; etc.—revealed that diasporas are mostly interested in investing in their own locality. The motivation towards investing in their own region can be attributed to the following factors:

Firstly, a constant tie with their own region helps them access the various environmental variables easily.

Secondly, they can observe the direct impact of their contribution and investment frequently, as and when they visit their own region.

China has been utilizing the potentials of its diaspora for the development of the country through Chinese and overseas centres. Chinese diasporic professionals have been providing teaching and various forms of training support back home to help enrich the specific regions they come from.[13] Similarly, the knowledge and talent base possessed by the Indian entrepreneurs in the UAE can be utilized to create business back home. For example, the diaspora belonging to Kerala has been investing in the betterment of their respective hometowns.

Remittance

Remittances are a stable source of external finance compared to private capital flow. Remittances sent to India by the working diasporas have increased. Ratha opined that "remittances are less volatile and may even rise—in response to economic cycles in the recipient country".[14] Capital flows increase during favourable economic condition and decrease during recession, whereas remittances remain more or less stable across time. According to the UAE exchange data the amount of remittances sent through the UAE exchange was Rs 193,322,082,896 in 2009, and a transfer of Rs 56,320,970,622 was recorded by the first quarter of 2010, which goes to show that despite recession, remittances have increased. The Indian diaspora in the UAE, owing to the temporary nature of their stay in the host country, are more willing to invest in their home country than foreign investors, "an effect that is similar to the home-bias in investment".[15] Even during recession, when they are forced to return to their homeland, as was seen especially in the case of the Indian migrants returning home from Dubai, they bring along their entire earnings and savings.

The role of remittance in poverty reduction has been supported by many authors. Richard Adams in his renowned work on remittance and poverty reduction stated that there is a statistical relationship between remittance and poverty trends. His analysis represents the fact that a 10 percent increase in remittance received from each individuals could help reduce poverty up to 3.5 percent. He conducted a survey on households in Guatemala and analysed the data to infer that International remittances reduced poverty here by 1.65 percent and the depth of poverty by 12.6 percent.[16]

The above discussion suggests that remittances made by the diasporas benefit all its recipients irrespective of their income groups. If this group could gain access to financial services, it could lead to further income generation.[17]

Impact of Remittance

Remittances are the main source of income for the families back home of the lower- as well as middle-income groups of the diaspora. It is a hard fact that many families are solely dependent on remittances for their basic needs and a major portion of these remittances is utilized for consumption alone.

This study emphasizes that remittance from the diaspora is a powerful economic resource, many labour-exporting countries have benefited through remittances in various ways. In 2002, $80 billion as remittance came into developing countries' funds which was used either to help poor families to sustain themselves or was paid as education or health expenses. In some cases it was spent on micro enterprises.[18] A number of studies[19] have acknowledged the fact that remittances were not only used for consumption but also in developing human capital, e.g. education, health and better nutrition. From an economic standpoint, the impact of remittance can be shown as follows:

Firstly, remittances from UAE to India have substantially increased the foreign exchange reserve.

Secondly, the number of blue-collar workers is higher in the UAE than skilled and semi-skilled workers. Most of these workers came to the UAE to escape from unemployment back home in India, since blue-collar workers are abundant in India.

Most of the Kerala migrants during their interviews commented that due to the geographical linkages with the UAE they preferred to come to the UAE than to the other neighbouring states. Remittances sent in by the Keralite diaspora in the UAE have played an important role in poverty reduction back home. "The larger the remittance, the higher is the percentage decline in poverty."[20] The multiplier effect of remittance cannot be denied. In fact it could stimulate demand for local production and services, thus generating employment and output, and a way out of poverty.[21]

Remittance has a positive impact on growth and investments as well. Most of the individuals interviewed during the course of this study had expressed their plans to start their own businesses back home. Though it was pointed out earlier that a major portion of remittances are not used for savings or investment, the remittances from the unskilled workers in the UAE have improved the standard of living for their families back home. In Kerala, nearly 70 percent of the remittances received is used either for home renovations or to buy new houses/plots of land besides other investments such as upgradation to household electricity (nearly 90%), LPG, consumer durables, etc. A major share of the remittance is spent on education. Reduced levels of poverty and insecurities have also boosted investments. Some studies have argued that these remittances have been widening urban-rural disparity as most of the investment is in real estate and takes place in the cities. McCormick and Wahbn stated that migrants returning to the Arab Republic of Egypt in 1988, had mostly invested in Greater Cairo. [22] "This may have been due to distortion in the economy that discouraged investments in rural areas."[23]

However, owing to the risks and uncertainties involved with investments, the diasporic Indian entrepreneurs have not taken much initiative towards investing in India.

Policy Recommendations for Remittance

A poor financial system discourages the remitter from investing and saving. As Johnson and Sedaca state, "One practical way to address poor access to financial services, while tapping into developmental potentials of remittances is to link remittances transfer services to financial services as a means to 'bank the un-banked' recipients. This process involves one-stop financial institutions that provide an easy and low-cost venue for migrants."[24] They pointed out that transfer operators like Western Union, Forex, Currency Bureau, etc., who engage only in cash transfers or exchange functions, cannot play a greater role compared to banks, credit union and micro finance institutions (MFIs). Banks and MFIs can provide other financial services such as savings accounts and loan accounts alongside transfer services. At the start, the recipients of remittances share a formal relationship with the banks but with time start opening bank accounts to keep the savings they make from the remittances. According to Johnson and Sedaca, "Financial institutions are more comfortable lending to remittance recipients who use their services since a regular stream of remittance payment can represent a form of future earning. In some cases, remittances could be used as collateral for lower lending rate." Orozco believes that this banking relationship can result in "financial democracy" whereby people of the lower income group can gain access to financial services. This will mean further income generation opportunities for many people.[25] Due to their close ties with the lower income group, MFIs are better placed to provide assistance to people belonging to the lower income group at a one-to-one level. Thus, strengthening the MFI capacity will bring about better results from remittance. In order to strengthen the MFI capacity, it is necessary to look at the following points:

1) There must be reduced transaction cost.
2) Financial services should be targeted towards unskilled and semi-skilled sections of workers through customized service.
3) Diasporic entrepreneurs should be encouraged to invest in Micro Finance.

Channelizing Remittances towards the Growth of Enterprises

In most countries growth in the private sector is constrained by lack of financial resources. Small- and medium-scale enterprises suffer from lack of seed capital and working capital. Remittances sent in by the diasporas and temporary labourers could help reduce these financial constraints if the accumulated savings could be invested properly. As we know, many migrants who do not stay permanently in the host country send a substantial amount of their income to their families back home. A majority, especially the Gujaratis and Keralites, want to invest in enterprises that will pay them back a good dividend, securing their futures for when they will have to return to their homes. Most of the migrants who have returned to Kerala have started their own businesses with their savings. Channelling remittances towards investments, irrespective of the size of the enterprise, will also generate employment opportunities.

"Nostalgic trade" refers to the export of traditional home/country products, such as fruits, coffee, pickles, sweets, etc., to meet the growing demand for these items among the immigrants settled overseas.[26] Production of such "nostalgic goods" in the home country for the diaspora overseas, a market many diasporic investors are interested to invest in, will bring about a social equilibrium in the overseas markets by meeting the demands. Motivating the diasporic entrepreneurs to invest in marketing these nostalgic goods will also increase the export earnings for the home country besides generating more employment opportunities. Al Maya Group, The LULU Department Stores run by Yusuf Ali, Al Adil Trading Co., etc., are examples of traders catering to the specific needs of the Indian diaspora in the UAE which show that the demand for Indian nostalgic goods have already motivated many entrepreneurs to invest in the UAE. An interesting aspect worthy of noting is that besides the target Indian diaspora, many fascinated foreigners are also regularly consuming these Indian items, and thereby creating more demand in the UAE market. The Indian entrepreneurs in the UAE are making the most of this market opportunity. Given the profitability in this market, these entrepreneurs should be proactively encouraged to invest in India by giving them better incentives. Finally, a "long-standing governmental diaspora outreach strategy" can further attract potential investors to the trade in nostalgic goods, especially from among the low- and semi-skilled diaspora group. Provided the level of awareness is increased among the potential investors, better results can be achieved.

Diasporic Entrepreneurs as a Source of Business Knowledge and Skill

The business diaspora could also contribute by:

a) being a role model for others to follow
b) transferring their various skills such as management, productive techniques, etc., which will bring efficiency and productivity.
c) facilitating the introduction of new products and technologies in the market; they can act as the "push factor" for bringing about various market reforms, provided their advice is taken into consideration.

In order to develop the link with diasporic entrepreneurs, various professional and business organizations need to be created. Through the presence of such networks, interested investors in the home as well as the host countries could gain knowledge about the prevalent business environment and other relevant information from the other side. The Indian Business Professional Group (IBPG), in Dubai, is busy creating such networks between various sections, with the intention of increasing the business traffic.

Role of Chambers of Commerce in Enhancing Diasporic Entrepreneurial Activities

The Chambers of Commerce can play a key role in enhancing trade, investments and other commercial activities. The Federation of Indian Chambers of Commerce and Industry (FICCI) has initiated an action plan to increase FDI inflow, whereby it has created a special division—the Diaspora Division—to serve NRIs (Non Resident Indians) and PIOs (Persons of Indian Origin). The main aim of the division is to leverage the diasporic trends towards India's growth.

"Pravasi Bharatiya Divas" is an annual convention held around January 9 each year, where Indian diasporas from various countries come together to discover and discuss various issues related to the diasporas. Though quite a few Indian entrepreneurs from the UAE—B.R. Shetty, J.R. Gangaramani, Mohan Jashanmal and Yusuf Ali M.A.—were honoured with the Padmashree Award at this annual convention, few interviewees commented that the small- and medium-scale entrepreneurs in the UAE get less attention and preference compared to the renowned ones. Such issues can only be addressed through proper dialogue.

Other than FICCI, Indian Investment Centre (IIC)—the governing body of India's Single Window Agencies—is engaged in attracting investments from NRIs and PIOs. IIC's main role is to provide guidance related to investments, joint ventures, technical collaborations, getting approval from government authorities, etc. In spite of such attempts, a major section of the diaspora in the UAE has expressed their dissatisfaction with the bureaucratic hassles they face from India. In order to enhance its role, the IIC should communicate with registered Indian associations like the IBPG, Indian Social Centre, Malayalee Samajam, etc., in the UAE to better handle diaspora-related problems.

Suggestions Regarding Investment Mechanism and Incentives for the Diaspora

James Rauch in his paper commented that membership of diaspora associations possibly increases diasporic contribution towards the homeland. These associations initially begin as social clubs. Later on these clubs form into professional associations that are capable of acting as a medium or link for international business activities.[27] Such associations might ultimately benefit India. Diasporic bonds and foreign accounts can attract more investment to the home country.

The role played by the diaspora in poverty reduction and economic growth has been the subject of interest among researchers recently. However, as previously mentioned, Indian policy makers have not been able to capitalize on the valuable resources in the possession of the diasporic entrepreneurs in the UAE and have failed to align them with the ongoing developmental programmes in India. The superlative achievements of the Indian entrepreneurs in UAE deserve due attention. Their contribution to the fields of business creation, simultaneous development of trade links, and the strengthening of bilateral ties between UAE and India cannot be ignored. Other than the financial impact through remittances and investments, the socio-cultural impact which they exert on their home country is also substantial. The Indian government has bestowed the Pravasi Bharatiya Award to many prominent Indian diasporic entrepreneurs in the UAE, in support of their unique capabilities as successful entrepreneurs, thus acknowledging the importance they are held in by their home country.

The subsequent suggestions propose various ways through which the resources in possession of the Indian entrepreneurs in the UAE can be utilized for further development by India. These suggestions are mainly based on knowledge gained from fieldwork and direct interviews conducted with a sample group of Indian entrepreneurs in the UAE. One of the main aims of this study is to narrow the information gap about the UAE and its economic environment amongst Indian policy makers. Looking from the perspective of UAE's economic potential, appropriate policy formulation targeted towards the diasporic Indian entrepreneurs in the UAE can yield highly favourable results. Most of the interviewees felt that the government of India formulated developmental strategies without any feedback from the overseas Indian entrepreneurs, rendering these strategies ineffective.

Development, in a broad sense, refers to economic growth, reduction of poverty, socio-economic equality and human empowerment. The greater Indian diaspora as well as the Indian entrepreneurs in the UAE can provide immeasurable support for various developmental activities in India. The geographic proximity between these two countries and the regular visits and contact shared by the diasporic entrepreneurs with their homeland makes it all the more easy. Also, the inherent sense of patriotism amongst the Indian diaspora in the UAE can trigger their motivation to associate themselves with various activities in India, if given due recognition.

However, despite the geographic proximity and age-old commercial relationship shared by the two countries, Indians have failed to fully penetrate the UAE market. The situation started to change after the oil boom with the Indo-UAE trade valued at around \$180 million per annum during the 1970s. The valuation today stands at around \$29,023.68 million. The UAE's emergence as a re-export centre has helped increase the scope of the Indian entrepreneurs. The commercial ties between the two countries can be enhanced if these entrepreneurs are utilized as agents for re-export. The Chamber of Commerce, IBPG Dubai, NORKA (Non-Resident Keralites Affairs, created by Government of India as a Special Department to overcome problems faced by the NRIs of Kerala) and all such institutions involved in the process should try to tap into the valuable resources of these Indian entrepreneurs. Appropriate programmes should be deployed to facilitate the participation of the Indian entrepreneurs in UAE in the re-exporting of Indian goods. The \$30 billion transshipment centre in Dubai with state-of-the-art facilities has attracted many investors to UAE. Dubai played a major role providing various goods to primarily three markets: Pakistan, Afghanistan and Iran. India should focus more on fostering the economic growth between India and UAE and availing the opportunities prevalent in this region. Our Ambassador to the UAE, Talmiz Ahmed, has rightly pointed out that Indian entrepreneurs in the UAE can act as the "lubricant in this field".

Indian policy makers should have a clear conception of their own preferential developmental needs and should try to find and utilize resources that are prevalent amongst the diasporic entrepreneurs in the UAE to that effect. Small- and medium-sized industries play a key role towards the equal distribution of wealth and economic growth. SMEs in India formed through funding and direct investment from Indian entrepreneurs in the UAE can act as a poverty-reduction engine for India. The Poverty Reduction Scheme initiated by the government of Ghana, which empowers the SMEs in the agro industry, can be cited as an example.[28]

Despite their various strengths, the SMEs face various crippling challenges such as poor finances, low levels of research and development, incapacity to adapt to changing circumstances, lack of trained human resources, lack of management skills and networking facilities, etc. Formation of SME clusters is necessary to minimize such difficulties; these could be linked to the Indian entrepreneurs in the UAE who can provide valuable guidance in the aforementioned weak areas. "Innovation and entrepreneurship hold the key to enhancing the role of SMEs in improving the Indian economy. As their importance is not well recognized, a country-wise program on entrepreneurship and innovation should be launched in the shape of national movement."[29] Entrepreneurs in the UAE should be encouraged to invest in SMEs. Their financial strength and international experience can be utilized for further growth in this sector. The Indian government has to take the initiative to create awareness among the UAE based Indian entrepreneurs about various policies related to this area.

According to Jayanta Roy and Pritam Banerjee, it is necessary to allow 100 percent FDI in small and medium industries.[30] Most of the successful entrepreneurs in the UAE are in the retailing business. By harnessing their expertise in this sector, a beneficial result can be achieved. The Indian government should focus more on the role of diasporic entrepreneurs rather than remittance and skill transfer. Looking at the future prospects in the UAE, an urgent action plan should be introduced so that the Indian entrepreneurs based there can play a bigger role. Any developmental programme is highly dependent upon popular participation from the people of the nation.

Critics have often claimed that the numbers and the size of Technological Business Incubators (TBIs) in India need to increase. The role of incubators is to support and nurture young firms. There are only about twenty incubators in India today as opposed to over a thousand in the US, three hundred in Korea and a hundred in Finland.[31] Engineering colleges and B-schools should launch programmes wherein the UAE-based Indian entrepreneurs can contribute. During their visits to their home country, they can offer technical support at the TICs (Technology Innovation Centres). These TICs which are normally located within the clusters of SMEs can generate an impetus to invest in their home country. According to Devesh Kapoor, the decision to invest in their homeland by the diasporic entrepreneurs is generated by non-pecuniary and emotional factors. Such factors motivate them to take higher risks to invest in their motherland. The Indian government has to channel these resources towards the cause by providing various supportive programmes.[32] The success stories of Indian entrepreneurs in the UAE can help nurture an entrepreneurial culture in India.

There are over 500 TICs which provide various kinds of support to SMEs in India. The UAE-based Indian entrepreneurs who are highly skilled can contribute towards business development and management through these centres. Multidisciplinary approaches should be initiated by the policy makers to utilize the resources possessed by the Indian entrepreneurs in the UAE.

Most of the Indian entrepreneurs in the UAE, especially the female entrepreneurs expressed their willingness to support the women's self help groups in India. Appropriate policy measures coupled with various incentive schemes and recognition programs can attract interest from entrepreneurs to invest in micro credit schemes.[33] Kerala's Global Support Network (KGSN), comprising eminent entrepreneurs, corporate executives and academics, can be cited as an example of a support network which should ideally be replicated in the other states of India too.[34]

Policies regarding remittances should focus on channelling them from consumption towards investment in other fields. Remittances are private funds, so only by initiating various innovative programs in consultation with the diaspora/diasporic entrepreneurs can the government provide proper guidance. Recent history shows that remittances, if channelled into micro credit schemes, help reduce poverty levels. According to Mohammad Yunus, the founder of Grameen Bank in Bangladesh and the father of micro finance, micro credit should target those facing problems with startup capital. He said that 5% of the micro finance bank clients manage to overcome poverty each year with help derived from micro credit services.[35] However, there remains one caveat—the bank should carefully judge the credit-worthiness of its clients.

The Indian Consulate and Embassy also has to play a crucial role in facilitating the link between the diasporic entrepreneurs and their home country. By collecting data on Indian diaspora/diasporic entrepreneurs, a quantitative appraisal can be assessed, which in turn will facilitate the matching of various needs of the UAE-based Indian entrepreneurs as well as their families back in their home country. Such a databank does not exist yet, but could be a valuable source of information for many sectors, if one is compiled eventually.

It has been pointed out earlier that compared to China, India has managed to attract significantly lower levels of FDI from its diaspora. China owes its success with FDIs to the strong network that exists among the diasporic entrepreneurial community that has effectively helped them reduce capital and marketing costs to boost the FDI inflow. In turn, these effects have also helped in minimizing transaction costs, thus enhancing cross-border trade. The reasons behind a rather modest inflow of diasporic FDI towards India are, but not restricted to, factors such as the below-par economic linkage and scarcity of small scale non-MNC entrepreneurs. Other than these, the primary defect expressed by the interviewees is the policy of reservation for several products for small- and medium-sized businesses. The Indian government should try to attract more FDI through a diasporic entrepreneurship program which will enable entrepreneurs in the UAE to invest in various productive sectors. The personal and social networks a few of these entrepreneurs belong to have greatly contributed towards this process.[36]

The Indian government has to collaborate with the entrepreneurs in the area of "social capital formation". The Dubai Shopping Festival is a good setting where the Indian government, in cooperation with the Indian diaspora, can create a better image of India. The knowledge possessed by the local entrepreneurs can be beneficial in strengthening the ties between the two countries. The Indian entrepreneurs can act as an engine for participatory growth provided they are given favourable conditions. While designing policies for diasporic entrepreneurship, policy makers should aim at removing the prevalent negative perceptions and stigmas about diasporic entrepreneurs and non residential Indians. As has been pointed out by Ram Buxani, such negative perceptions demoralize entrepreneurs and keep them from getting involved in programmes initiated by the Indian government.[37] As a result, they opt for humanitarian support such as foreign charities instead of contributing towards their homeland. In this aspect, the role played by the media could be paramount. In their interviews, the third generation Indian entrepreneurs in the UAE expressed their interest towards investing more in the home economy. Keeping them in mind, the Indian government has to identify and acknowledge the differences in the areas of interest, and deploy specific policies to remove barriers that may keep them from engaging in the Indian economy. Instead of pursuing a unified policy, the policy makers should initiate different approaches, empowering them to opt where they can contribute better.

To avoid unrealistic planning, it is necessary for a country to identify its own developmental needs and priorities, and accordingly ask the diasporic entrepreneurs in the UAE as well as local Indian entrepreneurs for their cooperation. A constant dialogue across the divide that exists between these entrepreneurs will help the Indian government identify the contribution each can make in terms of trade share, business creation and investment. The Indian government should also encourage regional and local projects where local agents can act as mediums providing supportive information. As Rao and Murthy pointed out, "Foreign investors have used the services of local agents for communication and for doing the initial 'spadework'".[38] Through these agents the investing entrepreneurs can gather information regarding the potential markets in other states, thus encouraging economic equality amongst the different regions in India.

Indian entrepreneurs in the UAE have historically been more successful than their counterparts of other nationalities. In order to attract more FDI and make the most of that resource, India should implement trade facilitation reforms. According to a recent WTO discussion, "trade facilitation" is "the simplification and harmonization of international trade procedure" covering the "activities, practices and formalities involved in collecting, presenting, communicating and processing the data required for the movement of goods in international trade." The role of trade facilitation is being given greater importance for attracting FDI and the resultant developmental growth. According to Jayanta Ray, "Trade Facilitation as an issue assumes added significance for Indian policy maker."[39] Meaningful trade facilitation will also motivate the UAE entrepreneurs to invest in small and medium enterprises based in India.

Various Indian entrepreneurs in the UAE have stated in their interviews that developed states are getting preferences for various investments. Though the responsibilities lie on the respective state governments to create a proper business environment, the central government can play an advisory role. According to Ogutcu, appropriate domestic policies will maximize the benefits from FDI which can help reduce impediments to local businesses.[40] According to Kundra, India's FDI policy is not decentralized like that in China; the policy is acting as a hindrance for effective competition among states, thus causing the urgent need for policy revision.[41]

The presence of several investment and trade promotion bodies may create inconsistencies in policy. Other than this, the barrier to investment in India, as stated by the interviewees, are as follows: lack of proper infrastructure, bureaucratic burden, lack of strong partnership, corruption, lack of appropriate support networks, unclear interlocutors at various governmental levels, and poor consular service. The Indian government must take appropriate measures to remove such impediments and match the resources of the entrepreneurs to the developmental needs of India.

Critics have pointed out that the Indian higher education system is not at par with the global levels, with the exceptions of IITs and IIMs. UAE-based Indian entrepreneurs who are engaged in the field of education, can be encouraged to invest in the education sector. Joint ventures in the education sector will benefit their home country as well as themselves. There is an urgent need for creating a favourable mechanism which will try to link similar kinds of entrepreneurs in India and in the UAE who can undertake partnerships and joint ventures.

The formation of an Overseas Indian Facilitation centre is a big step in the right direction that will help identify "the vast reserve of entrepreneurial talent" in the UAE. The primary roles it can play are:

a) Removing reservation policies for the small scale sector.
b) Focus on creating Freeport Zones for SMEs in India, like Dubai and Abu Dhabi.
c) Focus on retail sector where most of the UAE-based Indian entrepreneurs are successful.

Roy and Banerjee have recommended trade facilitation reforms in the following areas: port logistics, harmonizing standards, promoting business mobility and administrative transparency, professionalism, trade information, and e-business facilities. Unfortunately, all these activities are in a gestation phase. Speeding up the implementation of such policies will definitely yield positive results. Instead of projecting themselves as mere "talk shops", such institutions should employ a professional approach and prompt introduction of policies which will enable the Indian entrepreneurs in the UAE to become catalysts to the growth of their home economy.

ENDNOTES

1. Read the following works: Dilip Ratha, "Worker's Remittances: An Important and Stable Source of External Development Finance," *Global Development Finance* 2003, World Bank Report (December 2003); Brett Johnson and Santiago Sedaca, "Diasporas, Émigrés and Development: Economic Linkages and Programmatic Responses," U.S. Agency for International Development (USAID), Washington, D.C., Trade

Enhancement Service Sector (TESS) Project, CARANA Corporation (March 2004), http://pdf.usaid.gov/pdf_docs/PNADC365.pdf (accessed March 17, 2010); B. Lindsay Lowell and Stefka G. Gerova, "Diasporas and Economic Development: State of Knowledge," Institute for the Study of International Migration, Georgetown University, Washington, DC, World Bank Report (September 13, 2004), http://siteresources.worldbank.org/INTGEP2006/Resources/LowellDiaspora.doc (accessed March 17, 2010); Kathleen Newland and Erin Patrick, "Beyond Remittance: The Role of Diaspora in Poverty Reduction in their Countries of Origin," Migration Policy Institute, Department of International Development (July 2004), http://www.migrationpolicy.org/pubs/Beyond_Remittances_0704.pdf (accessed March 17, 2010).

2. P.R. Gopinathan Nair, "India," in *Migration of Asian Workers to the Arab World*, ed. Godfre Gunatilleke, 66–109, (Tokyo: United Nations University, 1986); Myron Weiner, "International Migration and Development: Indians in the Persian Gulf." *Population and Development Review* 8, no. 1 (March 1982): 1–36, repr. in *Indian Diaspora in West Asia,* ed. Prakash C. Jain (New Delhi: Manohar, 2007); K.C. Zachariah, K.P. Kannan and S. Irudaya Rajan, eds., *Kerala's Gulf Connection: CDS Studies on International Labour Migration from Kerala State in India* (Thiruvananthapuram: Center for Development Studies, 2002); K.C. Zachariah, B.A. Prakash and S. Irudaya Rajan, "Indian Workers in UAE: Employment, Wages and Working Conditions," *Economic and Political Weekly* (May 29, 2004): 2227–34.
3. Orozco, as cited by Dina Ionescu, in *Engaging Diaspora as Developmental Partners for Home and Destination Countries: Challenges for Policymakers* (Geneva: IOM, 2001), 23.
4. Ionescu, *Engaging Diaspora*, 40.
5. See the following works: B. Lindsay Lowell and Stefka G. Gerova, "Diasporas and Economic Development: State of Knowledge," Institute for the Study of International Migration, Georgetown University, Washington, DC, World Bank Report (September 13, 2004), http://siteresources.worldbank.org/INTGEP2006/Resources/LowellDiaspora.doc (accessed March 17, 2010); and, Robert E.B. Lucas, "International Migration Regimes and Economic Development," EGDI seminar Report, Executive Group on Development Issues. Stockholm, Sweden (May 13, 2004). http://www.egdi.gov.se/seminar6.htm (accessed March 17, 2010).
6. Deepak Nayyar, "International Labour Migration from India: A Macro-Economic Analysis," in *Kerala's Gulf Connection*, ed. K.C Zachariah, K.P. Kannan and S. Irudaya Rajan (Kerala: Centre for Developmental Studies, May 2002), 133.
7. Ionescu, *Engaging Diaspora*, 44.
8. Nirupam Bajpai and Nandita Dasgupta, "Multinational Companies and

Foreign Direct Investment in China and India," GCSD Working Paper No. 2, *Working Papers Series: Center on Globalization and Sustainable Development* (January 2004): 5, http://www.earthinstitute.columbia.edu/cgsd/documents/bajpai_mncs_china_india_000.pdf (accessed March 17, 2010).

9. Organisation for Economic Co-Operation and Development (OECD), *The Well-being of Nations: The Role of Human and Social Capital*, (Paris: OECD, Centre for Educational Research and Innovation, 2001), http://www.oecd.org/dataoecd/36/40/33703702.pdf (accessed March 17, 2010).
10. K.C. Zachariah, E.T. Mathew and S. Irudaya Rajan, *Dynamics of Migration in Kerala: Determinants, Differentials and Consequences* (Hyderabad: Orient Longman, 2003), 148.
11. Ionescu, *Engaging Diaspora*, 49.
12. *Ibid.*, 50.
13. *Ibid.*, 52.
14. Ratha, "Worker's Remittances," 161.
15. *Ibid.*
16. Richard Adams, "Remittances and Poverty in Guatemala," World Bank Policy Research, working paper no. 3418 (September 2004), 17.
17. Nathasa Iskander, as cited by Manuel Orozco, in "Worker Remittances: The Human Face of Globalization," Inter-American Dialogue, working paper commissioned by the Multilateral Investment Fund of Inter-American Development Bank (October 10, 2002): 26, http://www.focal.ca/pdf/remit_Orozco_worldwide%20remittances%202002.pdf (accessed March 17, 2010).
18. Carlo Dade, "Working with the Diaspora to Support Development," Inter-American Foundation, Paper no. 25 (August 2003). http://www.iaf.gov/publications/Fact_Sheets/2003_7_16_en/Remittances final2.pdf (accessed March 17, 2010).
19. Read the following works: Ratha, "Worker's Remittances"; Cerstin Sander, "Migrant Remiittances to Developing Countries—A Scoping Study: Overview and. Introduction to Issues for Pro-Poor Financial Services," report prepared for Department of International Development (June 2003); and, Tasneem Siddiqui and Chwodhury R. Abrar, "Migrant Worker Remittances and Microfinance in Bangladesh," report prepared for Social Finance Programme, International Labour Office (Februaury 2001) https://www.ilo.org/wcmsp5/groups/public/—ed_emp/documents/publication/wcms_117970.pdf (accessed March 17, 2010).
20. Zachariah, *Dynamics of Migration*, 257.
21. *Ibid.*, 268.
22. Barry McCormick and Jackline Wahba, "Return International Migration and Geographical Inequality: The Case of Egypt," *WIDER Research Paper*, no. 2004/07 (2004), http://www.wider.unu.edu/publications/

working-papers/research-papers/2004/en_GB/rp2004-007 (accessed March 17, 2010).

23. Ratha, "Worker's Remittances," 165.
24. Johnson and Sedaca, "Diasporas, Émigrés and Development," 80.
25. Iskander, as cited by Orozco, in "Worker Remittances," 26.
26. Eve Hamilton and Manuel Orozco, "Remittances, Diasporas, and Economic Development: Issues, Lessons Learned and Recommendations for Donor Interventions," USAID (November 2006): 35, http://www.docstoc.com/docs/42582616/REMITTANCES-DIASPORAS-AND-ECONOMIC-DEVELOPMENT (accessed March 17, 2010).
27. James E. Rauch, "Diasporas and Development: Theory, Evidence and Programmatic Implications," Department of Economics, University of California at San Diego (2003), 16–7.
28. Ionescu, *Engaging Diaspora*, 24.
29. Report of the Working Group on Science and Technology for Small and Medium Scale Enterprises (SMEs) for the Eleventh Five Year Plan, 2007–2012.
30. Jayanta Roy and Pritam Banerjee, "Trade Facilitation: The Next Big Step in India's Trade Reform," in *India's Liberalization Experience: Hostage to the WTO*, eds. Suparna Karmakar, Rajiv Kumar and Bibek Debroy (New Delhi: ICRIER and Sage, 2007), 17.
31. K.S. Chalapati Rao and M.R. Murthy, "Towards Understanding the State-wise Distribution of Foreign Direct Investments in the Post-Liberalisation Period," ISID Working Paper no. 2006/01 (April 2006), http://isid.org.in/pdf/wp0601.pdf (accessed March 17, 2010).
32. Devesh Kapoor, "Strengthening the Business Sector and Entrepreneurship in Developing Countries: The Potential of Diasporas," paper presented at United Nations ad hoc Expert Group Meeting, New York (October 5, 2006), 3.
33. Report of the Working Group on Science and Technology for SMEs.
34. Sunil Mani, Anjini Kochar and Arun M. Kumar (eds.), *Kerala's Economy: Crouching Tiger, Sacred Cows* (Kottayam: DC Books, 2006), 15.
35. *Gulf News*, August 1, 2009.
36. In an interview with Mohan Jashanmal.
37. In an interview with Ram Buxani.
38. Rao and Murthy, "Towards Understanding State-wise Distribution," 8.
39. Roy and Banerjee, "Trade Facilitation."
40. H. Christiansen and M. Ogutcu, *Foreign Direct Investment for Development: Maximising Benefit, Minimising Cost* (Paris: OECD, 2002): 4.
41. Ashok Kundra, *The Performance of India's Export Zone: A Comparison with the Chinese Approach* (New Delhi: Sage, 2002).

8

Role Models: Case Studies[1]

In its entirety, this study strives to represent the struggles and successes of the Indian diasporic entrepreneurs in the UAE. This chapter will be focussing on five of the most eminent business figures in the UAE—Jawaharlal R. Gangaramani, Yusuf Ali M.A., Bavaguthu Raghu Shetty, Mohan Jashanmal Jhangiani, and Ram Buxani—in an attempt to sketch out some role models for the coming generation of entrepreneurs and researchers.

JAWAHARLAL R. GANGARAMANI

Founder, President and Executive Chairman, Al Fara'a Integrated Group, UAE

Jawaharlal R. Gangaramani was born in Mumbai on December 22, 1949, and pursued civil engineering in college. He came to Dubai as a project engineer in 1974 to work on the Dubai World Trade Centre, at that time the tallest, "hi-tech" building being built in the Middle-East. He claims it was the challenge of working on this building project that bought him to Dubai. Soon after, he was appointed to work on the Al Ain flyover project. Thereafter, in 1980, he decided to invest his savings and establish a construction company of his own in Al Ain—he named it Al Fara'a Construction Company.

The success of the Al Fara'a Construction Company was largely based on their high standards of quality, service and timely delivery. Today, this group is regarded by the people of UAE as the one-stop shop for all sorts of construction requirements: civil engineering; ready-mix concrete; reinforced concrete structures; fabrication and erection of steel structures; manufacturing and installation of aluminium and glazed structures; as well as interior designing and installations.

Gangaramani believes that the future of construction companies lies in providing sustainable solutions and the Al Fara'a Group can be cited as a fine example. His goal is to achieve and maintain the Leed and Estidama ratings awarded for balancing environmental needs while catering to the needs of business realty projects.

A committed philanthropist, Gangaramani strives at all times towards giving back in more ways to the community. His efforts have been recognized by international communities over the years; he has been the proud recipient of the prestigious Padma Shree Award (January 2010) and the Pravasi Bharatiya Samman Award (January 2009) from the Indian government in the recent past. In his words, "I would not have been where I am today if it were not for the wisdom of the rulers of the UAE in creating an environment conducive to entrepreneurial success.¼ [this] land of opportunity [is] for anyone [who] is willing to work hard and pursue the vision of the Rulers of this great country."[2] Now he holds a UAE passport, a very rare honour for a person of foreign origin.

Al Fara'a Construction and Industrial Group: Company Profile

The Al Fara'a Group—a construction conglomerate with 24 companies in the UAE and India and a workforce of 20,000—has been operating in the UAE for the past thirty years. They offer world-class construction solutions to all kinds of businesses. Given the opportunities to work on high-class and challenging projects, Al Fara'a has remained the employer of choice for decades and still attracts the best of the professionals in the field to work for it.

The Al Fara'a Group has worked on several prestigious construction projects across Dubai and Abu Dhabi. Among its achievements are the Central Fish Market, Landmark Tower, and overlooking the Masdar City, the Eitihad Plaza (formerly known as Abraj Al Raha) in Abu Dhabi; and Ibn Battuta Mall, the Dubai Festival City, and Al Wheed Paradise Tower in Dubai. Le Grand Château, inspired by the Loire Valley in France and developed under the auspices of Al Fara'a Properties in the UAE, however, is Gangaramani's personal favourite.

In 2010, Al Fara'a completed three fruitful decades of service. With a philosophy of "excellence in partnership", a win-win approach to all negotiations and transparency in operations at all project phases, the Al Fara'a group has not only branded its own successes but also has succeeded in cajoling its clients, partners and suppliers into matching its levels of excellence. Thereafter, it has maintained the foundation of trust built in the process to ensure the best possible environment for collaborations. Hence, it does not come as a surprise that the Al Fara'a Group has managed to foster many dependable long-term employee relationships, and an enviable clientele in the UAE and the GCC region, some of whom have been with it for over a decade and yet some who have remained with the group since it started.

Today, the Al Fara'a Integrated Group is registered as the preferred supplier with all major public and private bodies in the UAE. Some of them are listed below:

The Planning Department of Abu Dhabi; Department of Social Services and Commercial Buildings; Abu Dhabi Public Works Department; The Private Department of the Ruler of Abu Dhabi; Etisalat; ADNOC; ADGAS; ADCO; Ewbank Preece Limited; Takreer; UAE Armed Forces (GHQ); Saudi Bin Ladin; Emirates Landscape; Al Aman Consultants

YUSUF ALI M.A.

Managing Director, EMKE Group, UAE

Yusuf Ali M.A. was born on November 15, 1955, to a trading family in Nattika, Thrissur district, Kerala. He did his schooling from Thrissur, but later moved to Gujarat, where he did his diploma in Business Managament and Administration. Thereafter, he left for Abu Dhabi in his prime, where he had landed a job for himself. Here he assisted his paternal uncle, M.K. Abdullah, Chairman and founder of the EMKE Group of Companies.

With the keen application of his knowledge of business administration and acumen for commerce it did not take long for Yusuf to assume responsibilities as the Managing Director of the EMKE Group. Amidst the raging turbulence of the Gulf War, when no one was willing to venture into the Middle East market with their businesses, with a firm faith in the principle that little is achieved without taking any risks, Yusuf took the bold step of introducing a chain of supermarkets in this region in 1990. In doing so, the firm strengthened its base among the middle-class Arabs and Asians in this region by providing the best buys and they also opened their own manufacturing units.

Besides, Yusuf was also instrumental in the construction of the Cochin International Airport at Nedumbassery, Kerala, in May 1999. This project, worth Rs 3.25 billion, "was initiated¼ [by] a company spearheaded by Yousuf Ali and a dedicated band of Non-residential Keralites (NRKs) [who backed] him in [this] Odyssey.¼ Contributions from Indians overseas, mainly Non-residential Keralites, from as many as 27 countries have gone into building the airport."[3] Today, he is on the Board of Directors of the Cochin International Airport.

Among his philanthropic contributions, he has been the forerunner in organizing timely relief measures from the Gulf during times of crisis in India such as the Gujarat earthquake, the Latur earthquake, and coastal tsunami tragedies. Besides, he contributed greatly to rehabilitating the Calicut market fire victims; as well as during the amnesty period in the UAE, he provided free air tickets and other facilities to Indians who could not afford a ticket to go back home.

Often referred to as the "unofficial ambassador of India to the UAE", Yusuf is ranked among the top NRI business figures in the world with his presence in India, Hong Kong, China, Thailand, Indonesia, Kenya, Benin, Tanzania, besides the Middle East countries. In recognition of his contributions to the society and achievements in business, Yusuf received the prestigious Padma Shree Award (May 5, 2008) and he was the first among the NRIs based in the Gulf and Middle East regions to have been felicitated with this award by the Government of India. He has also received the Pravasi Bharatiya Samman Award (January 2005), SIB Excellence Award (2009), Asian Business Leader of the Year Award (2007), Rajiv Gandhi Award (2006), and many other awards and felicitations. Being elected by the UAE business community as one of the members of the board of the Abu Dhabi Chamber of Commerce and Industry (ADCCI) could be described as the high point of his career. In addition to that, he was also elected Vice Chairman of the Trade Committee of the ADCCI by its board members.

EMKE Group: Company Profile

The EMKE Group was established by M.K. Abdullah in 1966 as an importer and wholesale distributor and re-exporter of dry foods, and later, frozen foods as well. Eventually, the business expanded to include a chain of supermarkets, departmental stores and hypermarkets. The group is home to a workforce of 20,000 employees of whom 13,000 are Indians while the rest are spread between 28 diverse nationalities. Today, under the leadership of Yusuf Ali M.A., the EMKE Group has enjoyed significant growth and diversified its operations into:

- Retail: shopping malls, hypermarkets, supermarkets and departmental stores, etc.
- Import and distribution, fashion apparel manufacture, food processing, etc.
- Export, IT education and training, travel and tourism, etc.

Retail business is the forte of the EMKE Group. They have spread their retail operations across the Middle East with manufacturing units established in parts of the Far East, India, Africa, and Guangzhou in China. Their Indian operations include food processing, exporting food and non-food products, and convention centres in Delhi, Lucknow, Mumbai, Chennai and Thrissur.

BAVAGUTHU RAGHU SHETTY

Vice Chairman and Managing Director, New Medical Centre Group (NMC)

Born into a backward family in a small village in India, Bavaguthu Raghu Shetty lived through the troubled realities of childhood in Indian villages, such as walking barefoot miles to school and back. He recalls being a rather mediocre child in school who had trouble reading and learning; however, he was hard working and dedicated. Today, his friends, staff, colleagues and competitors describe him as a living example of an individual honouring his Corporate Social Responsibility (CSR), a person whose rise to success is firmly anchored in humility and a sense of commitment towards the people around him and the society at large.

Having obtained a degree in clinical pharmacy in 1972, Shetty came to the UAE with just a few dirhams in his pocket. Over the course of time, he noted the underdeveloped state of healthcare in the new federation of UAE (formed in 1971) and decided to set up the NMC Hospital in Abu Dhabi, the first of its kind in the country. Later, branches were established in Dubai and Sharjah as well. This success led Shetty to carry out his diversification plans, foraying into a range of other businesses (see the NMC company profile below).

Business, however, has never been the real area of interest for Shetty, education being higher on the list of his personal priorities. To this end, he has established the largest community school in the region, assuming the position of the Chairman himself. He has also invested in a medical institution in the north Indian state of Uttaranchal, and is also on the board of directors of the Haldawni Medical College. He is also the founder and patron of the Indian Pharmaceutical Association in the Emirates. Besides, he was the president of the Abu Dhabi Cricket Council. He is also a member of the Advisory Board (Financial Sector), Economic Department, Government of Dubai, UAE, and the Pharmaceutical Committee, Dubai.

B.R. Shetty's biggest strength has been his resourceful family. He is married to Chandrakumari R. Shetty, who is a practicing doctor herself and is the Medical Director and Chief Medical Officer of NMC's healthcare division. They have four children together—three daughters and a son. The eldest daughter, Neema Shetty, is a dental surgeon and is married to a cardiologist, Sharad Shetty. Their second daughter, Reema, graduated with Business Management from Boston University and is a director at NMC. The third daughter, Seema, is a graduate in Science in Business Management from Boston University, with specialization in marketing and entrepreneurship. She is also a director at NMC and heads Zari Zardozi, an Indian themed restaurant in Abu Dhabi; and BiteRite, a food chain that specializes in food for diabetics with branches in both Abu Dhabi and Dubai. She also took over Aabharan Jewellery and in doing so changed the outlook of the jewellery industry in UAE. The youngest son, Binay, is a graduate in Finance and Entrepreneurship from Boston University with a presence in the Dean's list of outstanding academic achievements. He is also a director at NMC with his core attention focussed on Neopharma, a state-of-the-art pharmaceutical manufacturing unit in Abu Dhabi; besides, he is actively involved in the real estate and financial businesses owned by the NMC group.

Shetty's business achievements, philanthropy and other social endeavours have earned him innumerable prestigious awards and honours. In 2005, he was admitted to the "Order of Abu Dhabi", the highest honour awarded by the Government of Abu Dhabi, for his contribution to the development of UAE. He has also received the Padma Shree Award (March 2009), the Pravasi Bharatiya Samman Award (January 2007), and the Ernst and Young Middle East Entrepreneur of the Year Finalist Award.

New Medical Centre Group (NMC): Company Profile

The New Medical Centre, set up in 1975, were pioneers in providing modern medical services and supplies to the Gulf region. The group started business with NMC Healthcare, a pharmacy based in Abu Dhabi. In 1977, their flagship project, the New Medical Centre

Hospital was set up in Abu Dhabi. The hospital was the first of its kind in those days, fully equipped with state-of-the-art medical facilities all under one roof. Thereafter, NMC Healthcare remained invested in providing medical diagnosis, treatment and a range of healthcare services through their speciality hospitals, general hospitals and family clinics, set up all across the UAE. Today, the NMC group consists of:

- National Hospital, at Abu Dhabi; with Alternative Therapy Centre and Holistic Health Centre
- New Medical Centre, at Sharjah
- New National Medical Centre, at Mussafah
- Three NMC Speciality Hospitals, at Abu Dhabi, Dubai and Al Ain
- NMC Hospital, at Dubai
- NMC Family Clinic at Jumeirah.

Besides general diagnosis and treatment, the NMC Healthcare brand has been offering a wide range of speciality and super-speciality services in areas like Cardiology, Neurology, Gynaecology and Obstetrics, ENT, Orthopaedics, Laparoscopic surgery, Oncosurgery, Endocrinology, Ophthalmology, Urology, etc. For providing years of world-class treatment through its international hospitals and clinics, the NMC group received quality certification from the ISO 9001:2000 standards.

Earning an impeccable reputation as a world-class medical institution did not stop B.R. Shetty and the NMC group from diversifying into various other businesses such as pharmaceuticals manufacturing and distribution, scientific/medical equipments, financial services, engineering projects and services, gold and diamond jewellery, FMCG, foodstuffs, hospitality, advertising and public relations, real estate, IT, etc. Today, the NMC Group supports the livelihood of over 10,000 employees across its healthcare, finance, manufacture, IT and hospitality divisions. At present, Shetty and his group have ventured into and are sponsoring innovation in the fields of nanotechnology, biotechnology, cell therapy, and tissue culture.

MOHAN JASHANMAL JHANGIANI

Regional Manager, Jashanmal National Company, UAE

The fifth and youngest son of Hiro Jashanmal Jhangiani, Mohan Jashanmal Jhangiani belongs to one of the most respected business families in the UAE. Mohan Jashanmal was born on November 4, 1938. In 1949, he moved to Deolali, Maharashtra, India where he went to school. Thereafter, he went to Hoover Limited, in the UK, for training, set up workshops in Bahrain, Kuwait, Dubai, and Abu Dhabi between 1959 and 1964 and came to be known popularly as the "Hoover man in the Gulf".

He feels blessed and fortunate rather than guilty over having inherited the business empire created by his father. However, he too had to undergo a brief period of struggle before joining the Jashanmal Group. It was a rule in the family that each family member had to gather an initial three-year work experience working with one of their business partners before joining the family business. Mohan was sent to Hoover Limited, UK, to work as a mechanic.

In 1964, Mohan Jashanmal came to Abu Dhabi and took over as the manager of the Jashanmal Departmental Store and has been living there since. About doing business in UAE, Mohan's observation is that simply by talking straight and dealing transparently, and aligning one's long-term interests and prospects in business with one's UAE partner, one will have little to regret about doing business in the UAE. He has been an active agent in the formation of the Indian Businesses/ Professional Groups (IB/PG), one of the most active Indian business groups in Abu Dhabi, and served as its Chairman in 1992; he has twice accompanied the delegation of the Abu Dhabi Chamber of Commerce and Industry (ADCCI) on behalf of IB/PG to Canada and India. He was the Chairman of the Abu Dhabi Indian School in 1970. In 1965 he was one of the founder-members of the Indian Sports Club (known as the India Social Centre today) and has also served as the chairman.

Besides his father and brothers, he considers Thahil Thadani and Gangu Batra as his mentors and cites them among the reasons behind his success in life. Gangu Batra is the CEO of Jashanmal National Company and Mohan Jashanmal still works under and reports to him. Though he cannot read or write the language, Mohan Jashanmal can fluently speak Arabic. He is married to Maya Jhangiani and they have three children together. Their eldest daughter, Pushpa Jhangiani, owns the well-known Café Firenze in Khalidya. Their son Suhail and the youngest daughter are still studying in Boston and New York, USA. Owing to his high social standing, Mohan Jashanmal was granted permanent residency by the ruling family of Abu Dhabi. However, he has not given up his Indian citizenship, and the Jhangiani family does not require visas to visit India and Abu Dhabi.

Jashanmal National Company: Company Profile

Jashanmal National Corporation was founded by Rao Sahib Jashanmal Jhangiani in 1919 with his first general store in Basra, Iraq. The success of that store led the younger brothers of the family to spread out over the Gulf and set up branches wherever they found fertile soil, starting with Kuwait in 1934 where they found shopfront space on Safaat Square. Safaat Square was centrally located and a place for camel drivers to be hired for caravans, so the store saw a great deal of traffic. Narain Jashanmal set up the Bahrain branch in 1935, and Atma Jashanmal set up the Dubai branch in 1956 and it was managed by Hiro Jashanmal, Mohan Jashanmal's father, from 1958. In 1964 a branch in Abu Dhabi was set up, and the group began to diversify from its core sector of retail into wholesale, distribution and logistics. The group was formally incorporated in 1980 with Gangu Batra as CEO, thus bringing all the various limbs of the operation under one roof. The group expanded its operations to Oman and Qatar in 1990. From 2000 onwards, the group has had substantial interests in India. The group has two main branches: retail, which runs a chain of large-format department stores in the Gulf area carrying everything from luxury goods to toys and items of daily use, and wholesale, serving over 2,500 retail outlets around the Gulf region. The retail sector is the older one and is built on the foundations laid by Rao Sahib Jashanmal Jhangiani in the early twentieth century, while the wholesale operation represents the modern evolution of the philosophy of the early stores.

RAM BUXANI

Group President, International Traders (Middle East) Limited (ITL) Group

Ram Buxani was born in Hyderabad and went to school in Baroda. After the early death of his father, he had to start planning for his livelihood, which took him to typing classes after school. Soon he got a job at the institution where he used to learn typing. Later he came to Dubai, having found a job with International Traders (Middle East) Limited. He has been residing in Dubai for over four decades now.

Buxani was deeply influenced by the Japanese way of working that involves hard work and collective decision-making. He has played a key role in the interactions between the diasporic business community and the Indian Government. In recognition of his contribution he was awarded the *Bharat Ratna*: Man of the Year Award, awarded by *Bharat Ratna*, an English magazine published from Hong Kong. Among other honours earned by Buxani are: Citation by the President of India; the Jhulelal Award, from the International Sindhi Panchayats Federation; the Shiromani Award from the Association of Shiromani Awards; the Udyog Ratan Award, from the Institute of Economic Studies, New Delhi; the Overseas Indian Award, awarded by the Priyadarshini Academy; and the Bharat Gaurav Award, awarded by the Indian Merchants' Chamber, Mumbai.

In 2003, his autobiography, *Taking the High Road*, published in Dubai, was acclaimed by several critics.[4] This book not only presents an account of Buxani's struggles and successes, but also serves as a chronicle of the modern Sindhi community settled in Dubai, that has also seen him as a leading figure. A few years back, Buxani was also awarded a doctorate by the Washington International University, USA, for his study, "Governance in Dubai: The Influence of Tribal Tradition in Decision Making, Especially in the Critical Periods of the Development of the City-State". He was also presented with a second doctoral honour by the St. John's University, USA, in recognition of his autobiography.

Today, Buxani is one of the most respected business figures in Dubai. Among his many facets, he is a social organizer, a community leader, writer, actor, and a prominent spokesperson of the NRIs. He is a director at the Intro Group Limited and also at the Group President of the ITL (ME) Limited. He is on the Board of Directors of the IndusInd Bank Limited, India, and the IndusInd International Holdings Limited, Mauritius, and is the Chairman of Veeram International Limited. He is also a board member to the following companies: Tricolor Investments Limited; Al Razouki International Exchange Company, Dubai; Pure Ice Cream Company Limited, the makers of the "Kwality" brand of ice creams; Sanjay-Gulf Industries (Private) Limited, Punjab; and the Cosmos-Sanjay Textile Mills (Private) Limited, Punjab.

International Traders (Middle East) Limited Group: Company Profile

The group now known as ITL—International Traders Limited—was set up in 1953 in the pre-oil era, and it has flourished since. In 1958 it became the first incorporated venture in the UAE. The sector in which it operated was textiles. In those days of the Trucial States infrastructure was minimal, but the ITL group went forward in investing in Dubai's growth, a risk that paid off handsomely after the discovery of oil. One of the founders, Manghanmal Udharam, who later went on to be its chairman, became a major benefactor of the city of Pune in India, where he founded a college that is named after him.

The group was hugely successful in importing and selling textiles in the UAE, and this capital was ploughed back into manufacturing, wholesale and retail trade, and in 1960 into electronics. The electronics sector was then in its infancy in the UAE, there wasn't even a local TV station, yet ITL felt that it was the place to invest. This farsightedness also led it to move into chain retailing under the brand name Cosmos. The IT revolution followed and the consumer electronics segment blossomed. Soon ITL was offering a range of products related to photography, personal grooming, data management, foods and beverages, security, clocks and timepieces, home and kitchen goods, besides their core offerings of household and personal textiles.

The philosophy of the group remained that of calculated risk-taking, and loyalty to customers. Today ITL is part of the worldwide Intra Group, operating across Asia and Africa. It manages a network of more than 500 dealers in the consumer electronics segment all over the Gulf. Service and vision are their strengths. Since 2009 Dr Ram Buxani has been heading the group. His long experience and expertise in consumer electronics proved to be an asset to ITL, and he is taking the group forward into ever newer areas of innovation. Today, the ITL (ME)—International Traders (Middle East) Limited Group—has stakes in consumer electronics, textiles, banking and the hospitality industry.

ENDNOTES

1. Based on information received through individual interviews conducted by the author.
2. Maria Stapleton, "Incredible India: Construction Stalwart," India Review, *Middle East Interiors* 6, no. 3 (March 2011), http://www.middleeastinteriors.com/inhome.asp?articleid=1534 (accessed March 17, 2010).
3. N. Srinivasan, "Yusuf Ali: Flying High," Special Report, *Khaleej Times*, August 15, 1999.
4. Ram Buxani, *Taking the High Road* (Dubai: Motivate Publishing, 2003).

Bibliography

Abdulla, Abdulkhaleq. *The Arab Gulf States: Old Approaches and New Realities*. The Emirates Occasional Papers, no. 40. Abu Dhabi: The Emirates Centre for Strategic Studies and Research, 2000.

Abdullah, Muhammad Morsy. *The United Arab Emirates: A Modern History*. London and New York: Croom Helm and Barnes and Noble, 1978.

Abella, M.I. "Asian Migrant and Contract Workers in the Middle East." In *The Cambridge Survey of World Migration*, edited by R. Cohen, 418–23. Cambridge: Cambridge University Press, 1995.

"Abu Dhabi 2008–2009." Abu Dhabi Chamber of Commerce and Industry, and Information and Decision Support Center. 2008.

"Abu Dhabi: Business and Investment," Abu Dhabi Chamber of Commerce and Industry, and Information and Decision Support Center. 2008.

Abu Dhabi Marine Operating Company (ADMA-OPCO). *A Sucessful Journey through time, 1962–2007*. Abu Dhabi: ADMA-OPCO, 2007.

Adams, Richard. "Remittances and Poverty in Guatemala." World Bank Policy Research. Working paper no. 3418 (September 2004), 17.

Aggestam, Maria, and James J. Keenan. "Entrepreneurial Mindsets During Environmental Jolts: Vessels and Vaults." In *New Movements in Entrepreneurship*, edited by Chris Steyaert and Daniel Hjorth, 258–85. (Cheltenham, Glos: Edward Elgar, 2003)

Ahmad, S. Maqbul. *Indo-Arab Relations*. New Delhi: Indian Council for Cultural Relations, 1971.

Al-Abed, Ibrahim, and Peter Hellyer, eds. *United Arab Emirates*. Abu Dhabi: Trident Press and Ministry of Information and Culture, 1997.

Al-Ghufli, Saeed M.A.O. *Judicial Review of the Constitutionality in the United Arab Emirates: A Comparative Interaction*. Dubai: Dubai Police Academy, 2002–03.

Allen, Calvin H. Jr. "The Indian Merchant Community of Masqat." "The Indian Merchant Community of Masqat," *Bullettin of the School of Oriental and African Studies* 44, no. 1 (1981), 39–51. Reprinted in *Indian Diaspora in West Asia: A Reader*, edited by Prakash C. Jain, part 1: chapter 3. New Delhi: Manohar Publishers, 2007.

Al-Sayegh, Fatma. "Merchants' Role in a Changing Society: The Case of Dubai, 1900-90." *Middle Eastern Studies* 34, no. 1 (January 1998): 87–102. Reprinted in *Indian Diaspora in West Asia: A Reader*, edited by Prakash C. Jain, Part 1: Chapter 4. New Delhi: Manohar Publishers, 2007.

Al-Qasimi, Nora Muhammad. *The Indian Existence in the Arabian Gulf, 1820–1947*. Sharjah: Department of Education, 2000.

Amjad, Rashid. *To the Gulf and Back: Studies on the Economic Impact of Asian Labour Migration*. Geneva: United Nations Development Programme, 1989.

Annual Business Magazine. Business Monitor International. August 2007.

Anwar, M. "The Participation of Asians in the British Political System." In *South Asians Overseas: Migration and Ethnicity*, edited by C. Clarke, C. Peach, and S. Vertovec, chapter 13. Cambridge: Cambridge University Press, 1990.

Arasaratnam, Sinnappah. *Indians in Malaysia and Singapore*. London: Oxford University Press, 1970.

Bajpai, Nirupam, and Nandita Dasgupta. "Multinational Companies and Foreign Direct Investment in China and India," GCSD Working Paper no. 2. *Working Papers Series: Center on Globalization and Sustainable Development* (January 2004): 5. http://www.earthinstitute.columbia.edu/cgsd/documents/bajpai_mncs_china_india_000.pdf (accessed March 17, 2010).

Ballard, Roger. "Family Organization among the Sikhs in Britain." *New Community* 2, No. 1 (1973): 12–24.

———, ed. *Desh Pardesh: The South Asian Presence in Britain*. London: Hurst, 1994.

Baumann, Martin. "Diaspora, Generalogies of Semantics and Transcultural Comparison." *Numen* 47, no. 3 (2000): 313–337. Reprinted in *Sociology of Diaspora: A Reader*, edited by Ajaya Kumar Sahoo and Brij Maharaj, chapter 4, 63–77. Jaipur: Rawat Publications, 2007.

Beblawi, Hazem. "The Rentier State in the Arab World." In *The Arab State*, edited by G. Luciani. London: Routledge, 1990.

Bhagwati, Jagdish N., and Charles W. Calomiris. *Sustaining India's Growth Miracle*. New York: Columbia University Press, 2008.

Bhatt, C., and P. Mukta, eds. Special issue on Hindu Nationalism and the South Asian Diaspora, *Ethnic and Racial Studies* 23, no. 3 (May 2000).

Brown, R.A. "The Indian Political Elite in Malaysia." In *Indian Communities in Southeast Asia*, edited by K.S. Sandhu and A. Mani, chapter 9. Singapore: Times Academic Press, 1993.

Buxani, Ram. *Taking the High Road*. Dubai: Motivate Publishing, 2003.

Carland, J.W., F. Hoy, W.R. Boulton and J.C. Carland. "Differentiating Entrepreneurs from Small Business Owners: A Conceptualization." *Academy of Management Review* 9, no. 2 (1984): 354–59.

Chaudhri, K.N. *Trade and Civilisation in the Indian Ocean: An Economic History from the Rise of Islam to 1950*. Cambridge: Cambridge University Press, 1986.

Chell, Elizabeth, Jean Haworth and Sally Brearley. *The Entrepreneurial Personality: Concepts, Cases and Categories*. New York: Routledge, 1991.

Christiansen, H., and M. Ogutcu. *Foreign Direct Investment for Development: Maximising Benefit, Minimising Cost*. Paris: OECD, 2002.

Clarke, Colin, Ceri Peach, and Steven Vertovec, eds. *South Asian Overseas Migration and Ethnicity*. Cambridge: Cambridge University Press, 1990.

Cohen, R. *Global Diasporas: An Introduction*. London and Washington: University College London Press and University of Washington Press, 1997.

———, ed. *The Cambridge Survey of World Migration*. Cambridge: Cambridge University Press, 1995.

Dade, Carlo. "Working with the Diaspora to Support Development." Inter-American Foundation, Paper no. 25 (August 2003). http://www.iaf.gov/publications/Fact_Sheets/2003_7_16_en/Remittancesfinal2.pdf (accessed March 17, 2010).

Daniels, R. "The Indian Diaspora in the United States." In *Migration: The Asian Experience*, edited by J.M. Brown and R. Foot, chapter 4. Houndmills and London: MacMillan, 1994.

Davidson, Christopher M. *The United Arab Emirates: A Study in Survival*. Boulder: Lynne Rienner, 2005.

Davidsson, P., M.B. Low and M. Wright "Editors's Introduction: Low and MacMillan Ten Years on: Acheivements and Future Direction for Entrepreneurship Research." *Entrepreneurship Theory and Practice* 25, no. 4 (Summer 2001): 5–15.

Davis, K. *The Population of India and Pakistan*. Princeton: Princeton University Press, 1951. Reprinted by Russell and Russell, 1968.

Dobbin, Christine E. *Asian Entrepreneurial Minorities: Conjoint Communities in the Making of the World-Economy, 1570–1940*. Oxon: Routledge Curzon, 1996.

Drèze, Jean, and Amartya Sen. *India: Development and Participation*. New Delhi: Oxford University Press, 2002.

Economist, "Country Profile 2000: United Arab Emirates." *Economist Intelligence Unit* (2000): 4. http:// www.eiu.com (accessed March 17, 2010).

Elamandi, Abdulla. "India's Impact on the Gulf's Economic and Socio-Cultural Life During the British Era." In *Indian Diaspora in West Asia: A Reader*, edited by Prakash C. Jain, part 1: chapter 2. New Delhi: Manohar Publishers, 2007.

Federal Research Division, Library of Congress. *United Arab Emirates: A Country Study*. Washington DC: Federal Research Division, Library of Congress, 2005.

Fenelon, Kevin G. *The United Arab Emirates: An Economic and Social Survey*. London: Longman, 1973.

Freinkman, Lev M. "Role of the Diasporas in Transition Economies: Lessons from Armenia." *Cuba in Transition* 11 (August 2001): 332–42. http://lanic.utexas.edu/project/asce/pdfs/volume11/freinkman.pdf (accessed March 17, 2010)

Gandhi, Mohandas Karamchand. *The Story of My Experiments with Truth*. London: Jonathan Cape, 1966. First published by Penguin, 1927.

Ghosh, Biswanath, and M.V. Pylee. *Indian Ethos and Values*. New Delhi: Vikas Publishing House, 2010.

Grenier, Paola. "Social Entrepreneurship: Agency in a Globalizing World." In *Social Entrepreneurship: New Models of Sustainable Social Change*, edited by Alex Nicholls, 119–43. Oxford: Oxford University Press, 2006.

de Haas, Hein. "Engaging Diasporas: How Governments and Development Agencies can support Diaspora Involvement in the Development of Origin Countries." International Migration Institute. Oxfam Novib (June, 2006).

Hamilton, Eve, and Manuel Orozco. "Remittances, Diasporas, and Economic Development: Issues, Lessons Learned and Recommendations for Donor Interventions." USAID (November 2006). http://www.docstoc.com/docs/42582616/REMITTANCES-DIASPORAS-AND-ECONOMIC-DEVELOPMENT (accessed March 17, 2010).

Heard-Bay, Frauke, ed. *From Trucial States to United Arab Emirates: A Society in Transition*. Singapore: Longman, 1982. Reprint, London and New York: Longman, 1996.

———. "The Tribal Society of the UAE and its Traditional Economy." In *Perspectives on the United Arab Emirates*, edited by Edmund Ghareeb and Ibrahim Al-Abed, 254–71. London: Trident Press, 1997.

———. *The United Arab Emirates, A Quarter Century of Federation in Middle East Dilemma: The Politics and Economics of Arab Integration*. New York: Columbia University Press, 1999.

Helweg, Arthur W. *Sikhs in England: The Development of a Migrant Community*. New Delhi: Oxford University Press, 1979.

———. "Emigrant Remittances: Their Nature and Impact on a Punjabi Village." *New Community* 10, no. 3 (1983): 435–43.

———. "Social Networks among Indian Professionals in Australia." *New Community* 12, no. 3 (1985): 439–49.

———. "Why leave India for America? A Case Study Approach to Understanding Migrant Behaviour." *International Migration* 25 (1987): 165–78.

———. *An Immigrant Success Story*. Philadelphia: University of Pennsylvania Press; London: C. Hurst, 1990.

———, and U.M. Helweg. *An Immigrant Success Story: East Indians in America*. Philadelphia: University of Pennsylvania Press, 1990.

Henderson, Edward. *This Strange Eventful History: Memories of Earlier Days in the United Arab Emirates and the Sultanate of Oman*. Dubai: Motivate Publishing, 1988.

Herb, Michael. *All in the Family: Absolutism, Revolution and Democracy in the Middle Eastern Monarchies*. New York: Suny Press, 1999.

Hourani, George Fadlo. *Arab Seafaring: In the Indian Ocean in Ancient and Early Medieval Times*. Beirut: Khayat, 1963. First published 1951 by Princeton University Press, Princeton, N.J. 91.

Hudson, Michael C. *Arab Politics: The Search for Legitimacy*. New Haven: Yale University Press, 1977.

Hugo, G. "Migration and Development: A Perspective from Asia." *Migration Research Series* 14, IOM (November, 2003).

International Monetary Fund. "United Arab Emirates: Selected Issues and Statistical Appendix." *IMF Country Report*, no. 05/268. (August 2005).

Jain, Prakash C. "Indians Abroad: A Current Population Estimate." *Economic and Political Weekly* 17 no.8 (1982): 299–304.

———. *Racial Discrimination Against Overseas Indians*. New Delhi: Concept Publishing Company, 1989.

———. *Indians in South Africa: Political Economy of Race Relations*. New Delhi: Kalinga, 1999.

———. "Culture and Economy in an 'Incipient' Diaspora: Indians in the Persian Gulf Region." In *Culture and Economy in the Indian Diaspora*, edited by B. Parekh, G. Singh and S. Vertovec, chapter 5. London and New York: Routledge, 2003.

———. *Indian Labor Migration to the Gulf Countries*. Dubai: Gulf Research Centre, 2006.

———, ed. *Indian Diaspora in West Asia: A Reader*. New Delhi: Manohar, 2007.

———. *Non-Resident Indian Entrepreneurs in the United Arab Emirates*. New Delhi: Manak Publications, 2010.

Jain, R.K. "Culture and Economy: Tamils on the Plantation Frontier in Malaysia Revisited, 1998–1999." In *Culture and Economy in the Indian Diaspora*, edited by B. Parekh, G. Singh and S. Vertovec, chapter 3. London & New York: Routledge, 2003.

Johnson, Brett, and Santiago Sedaca, "Diasporas, Émigrés and Development: Economic Linkages and Programmatic Responses," U.S. Agency for International Development (USAID), Washington, D.C. Trade Enhancement Service Sector (TESS) Project. CARANA Corporation (March, 2004): 81, http://pdf.usaid.gov/pdf_docs/PNADC365.pdf (accessed March 17, 2010).

Kapoor, Devesh. "Strengthening the Business Sector and Entrepreneurship in Developing Countries: The Potential of Diasporas." A paper presented at United Nations ad hoc Expert Group Meeting. New York (October 5, 2006).

Kasim, Aqil. *The United Arab Emirates, A.D. 600 to the Present: A Socio-Discursive Transformation in the Arabian Gulf*. Dubai: Gulf Book Centre, 2000.

Kundra, Ashok. *The Performance of India's Export Zone: A Comparison with the Chinese Approach*. New Delhi: Sage, 2002.

Kurian, George. "Sociocultural Adaptation of South Asian Immigrants: The Canadian Experience." *The Journal of Sociological Studies* 6, no. 1 (1987): 47–62.

Lee Franklin, Robert. "The Indian Community in Bahrain: Labour Migration in a Plural Society." Ph.D Thesis, Harvard University, Harvard; University Micrifilm International, Ann Arbor.

Lele, J. "Indian Diaspora's Long-Distance Nationalism: The Rise and Proliferation of 'Hindutva' in Canada." In *Fractured Identity: The Indian Diaspora in Canada*, edited by S.J. Varma and R. Seshan, chapter 3. Jaipur and New Delhi: Rawat Publications, 2003.

Levi, Scotts Cameron. *The Indian Diaspora in Central Asia and its Trade: 1550–1900*. Leiden; Boston; Köln: Brill, 2002.

Lorimer, J.G. *Gazetteer of the Persian Gulf, Oman and Central Arabia*. Vol. 1: Part 2. Calcutta: Government Press, 1970.

Lowell, B. Lindsay, and Stefka G. Gerova. "Diasporas and Economic Development: State of Knowledge." Institute for the Study of International Migration, Georgetown University, Washington, DC. World Bank Report (September 13, 2004). http://siteresources.worldbank.org/INTGEP2006/Resources/LowellDiaspora.doc (accessed March 17, 2010).

Lucas, Robert E.B. "International Migration Regimes and Economic Development." EGDI seminar Report. Executive Group on Development Issues. Stockholm, Sweden (May 13, 2004). http://www.egdi.gov.se/seminar6.htm (accessed March 17, 2010).

Mani, Sunil, Anjini Kochar and Arun M. Kumar, eds. *Kerala's Economy: Crouching Tiger, Sacred Cows*. Kottayam: DC Books, 2006.

Markovits, Claude. *The Global World of Indian Merchants, 1750–1947: Traders of Sind from Bukhara to Panama*. Cambridge: Cambridge University Press, 2000.

McCormick, Barry, and Jackline Wahba. "Return International Migration and Geographical Inequality: The Case of Egypt." *WIDER Research Paper*, no. 2004/07 (2004). http://www.wider.unu.edu/publications/working-papers/research-papers/2004/en_GB/rp2004-007 (accessed March 17, 2010).

McDougall, P.P., and B.M. Oviatt. "International Entrepreneurship: The Intersection of Two Research Paths." *Academy of Mangement Journal* 43, no. 5 (2000): 902–06.

Meager, Carl. *Principles of Economics*. Translated by J. Dingwall, B.F. Hoselitz and Glencoe. New York: Free Press, 1950.

Miles, S.B. *The Countries and Tribes of the Persian Gulf*. London: Frank Cass, 1966.

Milne, Alan Alexander. *Winnie-the-Pooh*. London: Methuen & Co., 1926.

Ministry of Information and Culture, UAE. *The United Arab Emirates: An Ancient People and a Young Country*. Abu Dhabi: Ministry of Information and Culture, 1992.

Motwani, Jagat K., Mahin Gosine and Jyoti Barot Motwani, eds. *Global Indian Diaspora: Yesterday, Today and Tomorrow*. New York: *Global* Organization of People of Indian Origin, 1993.

Mullo, Anand. *Voices of the Indian Diaspora*. Delhi: Motilal Banarsidass, 2007.

Nair, P.R. Gopinathan. "India." In *Migration of Asian Workers to the Arab World*, edited by Godfre Gunatilleke, 66–109. Tokyo: United Nations University, 1986.

———. "Incidence, Impact and Implications of Migration to the Middle East from Kerala (India)." In *To the Gulf and Back: Studies on the Economic Impact of Asian Labour Migration*, edited by Rashid Amjad, 343–64. New Delhi: ILO-Artep, 1989.

———. "Migration of Keralites to the Arab World." In *Kerala's Economy: Performance, Problems, Prospects*. New Delhi: Sage Publications, 1994.

Nayyar, Deepak. *Migration, Remittances and Capital Flows: The Indian Experience*. Delhi: Oxford University Press, 1994.

———. *Governing Globalization: Issues and Institutions*. Oxford: Oxford University Press, 2002.

———. "International Labour Migration from India: A Macro-Economic Analysis." In *Kerala's Gulf Connection*, edited by K.C. Zachariah, K.P. Kannan and S. Irudaya Rajan. Kerala: Centre for Developmental Studies, May 2002.

Newland, Kathleen, and Erin Patrick. "Beyond Remittance: The Role of Diaspora in Poverty Reduction in their Countries of Origin." Migration Policy Institute. Department of International Development (July, 2004). http://www.migrationpolicy.org/pubs/Beyond_Remittances_0704.pdf (accessed March 17, 2010).

———, and Hiroyuki Tanaka, "Mobilizing Diaspora: Entrepreneurship for Development." Migration Policy Institute. U.S. Agency for International Development (USAID). Washington, D.C. (October, 2010).

Organisation for Economic Co-Operation and Development (OECD). *The Well-being of Nations: The Role of Human and Social Capital*. Paris: OECD, Centre for Educational Research and Innovation, 2001. http://www.oecd.org/dataoecd/36/40/33703702.pdf (accessed March 17, 2010).

Orozco, Manuel. *Remittances to Latin America and the Carribean: Issues and Perspectives on Development*. Organization of American States Report (September, 2004).

———, "Worker Remittances: The Human Face of Globalization," Inter-American Dialogue. Working paper commissioned by the Multilateral Investment Fund of Inter-American Development Bank (October 10, 2002): 26. http://www.focal.ca/pdf/remit_Orozco_worldwide%20remittances%20 2002.pdf (accessed March 17, 2010).

Parekh, B. *Some Reflections on the Indian Diaspora*. London: British Organisation of People of Indian Origin (BOPIO), 1993.

———, Singh, G. and Vertovec, S., eds. *Culture and Economy in the Indian Diaspora*. London and New York: Routledge, 2003.

Rao, K.S. Chalapati, and M.R. Murthy. "Towards Understanding the State-wise Distribution of Foreign Direct Investments in the Post-Liberalisation Period." ISID Working Paper no. 2006/01 (April 2006). http://isid.org.in/pdf/wp0601.pdf (accessed March 17, 2010).

Ratha, Dilip. "Worker's Remittances: An Important and Stable Source of External Development Finance." *Global Development Finance 2003*, World Bank Report (December 2003).

Rauch, James E. "Diasporas and Development: Theory, Evidence and Programmatic Implications." Department of Economics, University of California at San Diego, 2003.

Robinson, V. "Boom and Gloom: The Success and Failure of South Asians in Britain." In *South Asians Overseas: Migration and Ethnicity*, edited by C. Clarke, C. Peach and S. Vertovec, chapter 12. Cambridge: Cambridge University Press, 1990.

———. "The Migration of East African Asians to the UK." In *The Cambridge Survey of World Migration*, edited by R. Cohen, 331–36. Cambridge: Cambridge University Press, 1995.

Roy, Jayanta, and Pritam Banerjee. "Trade Facilitation: The Next Big Step in India's Trade Reform." In *India's Liberalization Experience: Hostage to the WTO*, edited by Suparna Karmakar, Rajiv Kumar and Bibek Debroy. New Delhi: ICRIER and Sage, 2007.

Sahoo, Ajaya Kumar, and Brij Maharaj, eds. *Sociology of Diaspora: A Reader*. Jaipur: Rawat Publications, 2007.

Sander, Cerstin. "Migrant Remiittances to Developing Countries—A Scoping Study: Overview and. Introduction to Issues for Pro-Poor Financial Services." A report prepared for Department of International Development (June 2003).

Sandhu, K.S., and A. Mani, eds. *Indian Communities in Southeast Asia*. Singapore: Times Academic Press, 1993.

Schumpeter, Joseph A. *The Theory of Economic Development*. Cambridge, MA: Harvard University Press, 1934.

———. "*Capitalism, Socialism and Democracy*. London: George Allen and Unwin, [1943] 1976).

Sekhar, T.V. "Migration Selectivity from Rural Areas: Evidences from Kerala." *Demography India* 22, no. 2 (1993): 191–202.

———. "Male Emigration and Changes in the Family: Impact on Female Sex Roles." *Indian Journal of Social Work* 57, no. 2 (1996): 277–94.

Sheffer, Gabriel. "The Emergence of New Ethno-National Diasporas." *Migration: A European Journal of International Migration and Ethnic Relations* 28, no. 2 (1995): 5–28. Reprinted in *Sociology of Diaspora: A Reader*, edited by Ajaya Kumar Sahoo and Brij Maharaj, 43–60. Jaipur: Rawat Publications, 2007.

Shuval, Judith T. "Diaspora Migration: Definitional Ambiguities and a Theoretical Paradigm." *International Migration* 38, no. 5 (2000): 41–57. Reprinted in *Sociology of Diaspora: A Reader*, edited by Ajaya Kumar Sahoo and Brij Maharaj, 29–41. Jaipur: Rawat Publications, 2007.

Siddique, Sharon, and Nirmala Purushottam. *Singapore's Little India: Past, Present, and Future*. Singapore: Institute of South-East Asian Studies, 1982.

Singer, Philip. "Caste and Identity in Guyana." In *Caste in Overseas Indian Communities*, edited by Barton M. Schwartz, 93–116. San Francisco: Chandler, 1967.

Singh, I.J. Bahadur, ed. *The Other India: The Overseas Indians and Their Relationship with India*, proceedings of a seminar. New Delhi: Arnold-Heinemann, 1979.

———, ed. *Indians in South-East Asia*. New Delhi: Sterling Publishers, 1982.

———, ed. *Indians in South Asia*. New Delhi: Sterling Publishers, 1984.

———, ed. Indians in the Caribbean. New Delhi: Sterling Publishers, 1987.

Siu, Paul C.P. "The Sojourner." *The American Journal of Sociology* 58, no. 1 (1952): 34–44.

Smith, Michael, and Alexis Waller. "Recent Development in UAE Property Law." *Economic Focus*, Arab-British Chamber of Commerce Publications (September 2007). Published online by *Clyde and Co.* http://www.clydeco.com/knowledge/articles/recent-developments-in-uae-property-law.cfm (accessed February 15, 2009).

Smith, Raymond T. "Ethnic Difference and Peasant Economy in British Guiana." In *Capital, Saving and Credit in Peasant Societies*, edited by Raymond Firth and B.S. Yamey, 305–29. London: George Allen and Unwin, 1964.

———, "Race and Political Conflict in Guyana." *Race* 12, no. 4 (1971): 415–27.

———, *The Matrifocal Family: Power, Pluralism and Politics*. New York/London: Routledge, 1996.

———, and Chandra Jayawardena. In *Caste in Overseas Indian Communities*, edited by Barton M. Schwartz, 43–92. San Francisco: Chandler, 1967.

Solimino, A. "Globalising Talent and Human Capital." A paper presented at *Implication for Developing Countries*, ABCDE Conference for Europe, Oslo, 2002.

Srinivasan, N. "Yusuf Ali: Flying High." Special Report, *Khaleej Times*. August 15, 1999.

Stapleton, Maria. "Incredible India: Construction Stalwart." India Review, *Middle East Interiors* 6, no. 3 (March 2011), http://www.middleeastinteriors.com/inhome.asp?articleid=1534 (accessed March 17, 2010).

Stoner, James A.F., R.E. Freeman and D.R. Gilbert Jr. *Management*. New Delhi: Prentice Hall of India Private Limited, 2001.

Sundaram, Vasanti. *Footprints: Memoirs of an Indian Patriarch*. Dubai: Motivate Publishing, 2009.

Tambiah, Stanley J. "Transnational Movement, Diaspora, and Multiple Modernities." *Dædalus* 129, No 1 (Winter 2000): 163–94.

Tatla, Darshan Singh. *The Sikh Diaspora: The Search for Statehood*. Seattle: University of Washington Press, 1999.

Thakur, Andra P. "The Impact of Emigration and Remittances on an Indo-Guyanese Village Economy in Guyana." *Indo Caribbean Review* 2, No. 2 (1995): 105–25.

Tinker, H. *A New System of Slavery: The Export of Indian Labour Overseas, 1830–1920*. London: Oxford University Press, 1974.

———. *The Banyan Tree: Overseas Emigrants from India, Pakistan and Bangladesh*. Oxford: Oxford University Press, 1977.

Tölölyan, Khachig. "The Nation-State and its Others: In Lieu of a Preface." *Diaspora* 1, No. 1 (1991): 3–7. Reprinted in *Sociology of Diaspora: A Reader*, edited by Ajaya Kumar Sahoo and Brij Maharaj. Jaipur: Rawat Publications, 2007.

Tripathi, Dwizendra. "An Integrated view of Entrepreneurship." *Economic and Political Weekly* 20, No. 48 (November 30, 1985): 163–68. www.jstor.org/stable437057 (accessed July 21, 2009).

Tsagarousianou, Roza. "Rethinking the Concept of Diaspora: Mobility, Connectivity and Communication in a Globalised World." *Westminster Papers in Communication and Culture* 1, No. 1 (2004): 52–66.

Turner, Jonathan H., and Edna Bonacich. "Toward a Composite Theory of Middlemen Minorities." *Ethnicity* 7, No. 2 (1980): 144–58.

"UAE Business Forecast Report: Q1 2009," Business Monitor International (October 2008).

Vanderveer, P., ed. *Nation and Migration: The Politics of Space in the South Asian Diaspora*. Philadelphia: University of Pennsylvania Press, 1995.

Visram, R. Ayahs, and Lascars Princes. *Indians in Britain, 1700–1947*. London: Pluto Press, 1986.

Vivekanand, P.V. *Pearl of Dubai*. Dubai, UAE: Quality Printing Service, 2008.

Walton-Roberts, Margaret. "Globalisation National Autonomy and Non-Resident Indians." *Contemporary South Asia* 13, No. 1 (March 2004): 53–69.

Weiner, Myron. "International Migration and Development: Indians in the Persian Gulf." *Population and Development Review* 8, No. 1 (March 1982): 1–36. Reprinted in *Indian Diaspora in West Asia,* edited by Prakash C. Jain, 127–76. New Delhi: Manohar, 2007.

Williams, R.B., ed. *A Sacred Thread: Modern Transmission of Hindu Tradition in India and Abroad*. Chambersburg: Anima, 1992.

Zachariah, K.C., E.T. Mathew, and S. Irudaya Rajan. *Dynamics of Migration in Kerala: Determinants, Differentials and Consequences*. New Delhi: Orient Longman, 2003.

———, K.P. Kannan and S. Irudaya Rajan, eds. *Kerala's Gulf Connection: CDS Studies on International Labour Migration from Kerala State in India*. Thiruvananthapuram: Center for Development Studies, 2002.

———, B.A. Prakash and S. Irudaya Rajan. "Indian Workers in UAE: Employment, Wages and Working Conditions." *Economic and Political Weekly* (May 29, 2004): 2227–34.

Zahlan, Rosemarie Said. *The Origins of UAE: Political and Social History of the Trucial States*. London: Macmillan, 1978.

———. *The Making of the Modern Gulf States: Kuwait, Bahrain, Qatar, the United Arab Emirates and Oman*, London: Unwin Hyman Ltd, 1989; reprint, Ithaca, 1998.

Index